Everym S

CONTENTS

Welcome to Venice!
This opening fold-out contains a general map of Venice to help you visualise the 6 large districts discussed in this guide, and 4 pages of valuable information, handy tips and useful addresses.

Discover Venice through 6 districts and 6 maps
A Piazza San Marco/ Castello (southwest)
B San Marco / Accademia / Dorsoduro (east)
C Dorsoduro (west)
D Rialto / San Polo / Santa Croce
E Cannaregio / Ghetto Nuovo
F Fondamenta Nuove / Castello (north)

For each district there is a double-page of addresses (restaurants – listed in ascending order of price – cafés, bars, music venues and shops) followed by a fold-out map for the relevant area with the essential places to see (indicated on the map by a star ★). These places are by no means all that Venice has to offer but to us they are unmissable. The grid-referencing system (**A** B2) makes it easy for you to pinpoint addresses quickly on the map.

Transport and hotels in Venice
The last fold-out consists of a transport map and 4 pages of practical information that include a selection of hotels.

Thematic index
Lists all the sites and addresses featured in this guide.

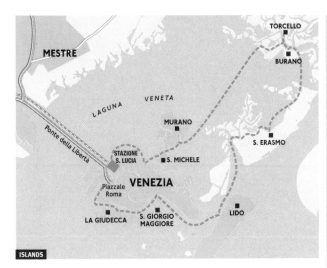

→ Lido 136/ B, via Sandro Gallo
Tel. 041 526 57 42
Take a rowing trip Venice-style – standing up. Lessons for beginners.

With a guide
Associazione Guide Turistiche (A B1)
→ Castello, Calle Cassellaria, 5327 Tel. 041 520 90 38
Price 110 € per group
Guided tours around Venice in different languages.

SHOPPING

Opening times
Generally Mon-Sat 9am–12.15pm, 3–7.30pm. In high season shops open all day every day.
Sales
Twice yearly: winter (Jan-Feb) and summer (July-Aug).
Department stores
Coin (**D** F3)
→ Cannaregio, Salizzada San Giovanni Crisostomo, 5787
Tel. 041 520 35 81

Standa (**D** E1)
→ Cannaregio, Strada Nuova, 3659
Tel. 041 523 80 46
Fashion
Outlets of the leading Italian designer labels.
La Coupole (**B** E2)
→ San Marco, Calle Larga XXII Marzo, 2031
Collections by various designers.
Laura Biagiotti (**B** E2)
→ San Marco, Calle Larga XXII Marzo, 2400
Missoni (**A** A3)
→ San Marco, Calle Vallaresso, 1312/ B
Emporio Armani (**A** A2)
→ San Marco, Calle dei Fabbri, 989

MARKETS

Rialto
This former merchant district is still home to the majority of the city's markets.
→ Erberia, San Polo (**D** F3)

Mon-Sat 7am–1pm
Fruit and vegetables.
→ Campo della Pescaria, San Polo (**D** E2)
Tue-Sat 5–11.30am
Fish.
Via Garibaldi
→ Castello, Mon-Sat
Floating vegetable market on the canal, situated at the end of the street, close to the Arsenal.
Campo Santa Margherita (**C** E2)
→ Daily, mornings only
Small fish market, and fruit and vegetables.

RESTAURANTS

The menu
Traditional meals are large: following the antipasti are two main courses, the primo piatto (usually pasta or risotto), and the secondo (meat or fish) with contorni (vegetables), followed by dolce (dessert). Today, it is usual to order only one

CHIC VENICE

San Marco
All the big names in designer fashions around the Calli Vallaresso (**A** A3) and Larga XXII Marzo (**B** F2).
Campo Santo Stefano (**B** C2)
The best shops for souvenirs and elegant gifts are located around this beautiful Campo.
La Fenice (**B** E2)/ **Campo San Maurizio** (**B** D2)
The main district for antiques shops.

ETERNAL VENICE

Piazza San Marco (**A** B2)
Between Palazzo Ducale (Doge's Palace) and the basilica.
The Grand Canal
The main waterway through the city, bordered by 100 palaces.
Rialto Bridge (**D** F3)
This old, arcaded stone bridge is lined with shops on both sides.
La Fenice (**B** E2)
Opera house, still being rebuilt after the 1996 fire.
Bridge of Sighs (**A** C2)
Once the condemned man's route to prison, now the bridge of lovers.

WRITER'S VENICE

Reminders of **Goldoni** at Palazzo Centani, **George Sand**'s signature at Danieli-Sandwirth, **Kafka**'s at Gabrielli-Sandwirth, the ghost of **Thomas Mann** at the Grand Hotel and the Lido baths, the tomb of **Ezra Pound** at San Michele, **Balzac**'s table at Florian and **Hemingway**'s at Harry's Bar.

Welcome to Venice!

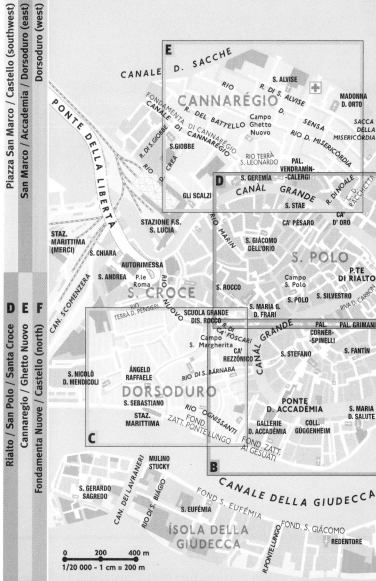

A — Piazza San Marco / Castello (southwest)
B — San Marco / Accademia / Dorsoduro (east)
C — Dorsoduro (west)
D — Rialto / San Polo / Santa Croce
E — Cannaregio / Ghetto Nuovo
F — Fondamenta Nuove / Castello (north)

E — CANALE D. SACCHE

CANNARÉGIO

RIO — S. ALVISE — R. DI S. ALVISE — MADONNA D. ORTO

FONDAMENTA CANALE DI CANNARÉGIO — R. DEL BATTELLO — Campo Ghetto Nuovo — SENSA — SACCA DELLA MISERICÓRDIA

R. DI S. GIOBBE — RIO — D. CREA — S.GIOBBE — RIO TERRÀ S. LEONARDO — RIO D. MISERICÓRDIA

PAL. VENDRAMIN-CALERGI

D — S. GEREMÍA — CANÀL GRANDE — R. DI NOALE — C. D. RACCHETTA

GLI SCALZI — S. STAE — CA' D'ORO

STAZIONE F.S. S. LUCIA — CA' PÉSARO

RIO MARIN — S. GIÁCOMO DELL'ORIO — S. POLO

STAZ. MARÍTTIMA (MERCI) — S. CHIARA

AUTORIMESSA — P.le Roma — S. ANDREA — P.TE DI RIALTO

CAN. SCOMENZERA — RIO NUOVO — S. CROCE — S. ROCCO — Campo S. Polo — S. POLO — S. SILVESTRO — RIVA DEL CARBON

RIO TERRÀ D. PENSIERI — SCUOLA GRANDE DIS. ROCCO — S. MARIA G. D. FRARI

RIO DI S. FOSCARI — PAL. CORNÉR-SPINELLI — PAL. GRIMANI

S. NICOLÒ D. MENDICOLI — ÁNGELO RAFFAELE — Campo S. Margherita — CA' REZZÓNICO — S. STEFANO — S. FANTÍN

S. SEBASTIANO — RIO DI S. BÁRNABA — DORSODURO — CANÀL GRANDE

STAZ. MARÍTTIMA — RIO OGNISSANTI — FOND. ZATT. PONTE LUNGO — PONTE D. ACCÁDEMIA — S. MARIA D. SALUTE

GALLERIE D. ACCÁDEMIA — COLL. GÚGGENHEIM — FOND. ZATT. AI GESUATI

B

MULINO STUCKY — CAN. DEI LAVRANERI — FOND. S. EUFÉMIA

S. GERARDO SAGREDO — RIO DI S. BIÁGIO — S. EUFÉMIA — FOND. S. GIÁCOMO

ÍSOLA DELLA GIUDECCA — FOND. PONTE LUNGO — REDENTORE

CANALE DELLA GIUDECCA

0 — 200 — 400 m
1/20 000 - 1 cm = 200 m

BRIDGE OF SIGHS

GONDOLAS

CITY PROFILE

- 6 districts or *sestieri*
- 1,375 acres ■ 76,000 inhabitants; 300,000 including the suburbs
- 1.3 million visitors each year ■ 160 canals; the main one being the Grand Canal: 1.5 miles long and 76.5 yds wide.

VIEWS OF VENICE

Campanile della Piazza San Marco (**A** B2)
The highest: a 320ft-high view of the city, the San Marco basin and the islands of the lagoon.
Ponte di Rialto / Rialto Bridge (**D** F3)
The most famous: just above the Grand Canal.
Vaporetto line no. 1
The most impressive: a view of the 100 palaces along the Grand Canal.
Zattere (**B** D4)
The best of the Lagoon: the old quays, view of the islands of the Giudecca and San Giorgio Maggiore.

THE EURO €

Check the Euro exchange rate with your bank/travel agent before departure.

GREEN SPACES

Opening times
From sunrise to sunset.
Parks and gardens
There are parks all over the city, as well as gardens and grounds attached to villas and palaces.
Giardini Pubblici
→ *Castello;*
Vaporetto: Giardini
The foremost public garden in Venice, located around the Biennale pavilions.
Parco Savorgnan (**E** B3)
→ *Cannaregio,*
Fondamenta Venier 348–9
The oldest garden in the city, first laid out in the 12th century and then redesigned as an English-style garden in the 1700s.
Giardino Papadopoli

→ *Santa Croce;*
Vaporetto: Piazzale Roma
Garden dating from 1810, behind Piazzale Roma. Lovely views over the Grand Canal.
Giardini ex Reali (**A** A3)
→ *San Marco,*
Riva Degli Schiavoni
Napoleon's royal gardens, behind the Procuratie Nuove.

TOWARD THE ISLANDS

Discover the hidden treasures of Venice's Lagoon.
Boat trips
Centro Internazionale Città d'acqua
→ Tel. 041 523 04 28
Mon-Fri 9am–6.30pm
Organizes guided tours of the main islands of the Lagoon.
La Giudecca
→ *Motoscafi n° 41/42, 82*
Looking across to Venice,

a calmer, more residential district.
San Giorgio Maggiore
→ *Vaporetto n° 82*
The island of cypress trees. From the top of the church campanile are unobstructed views of Venice and the islands.
The Lido
→ *Line n° 1, 6, 14, 51/52, 61/62 and 82*
The island of the stars, with 7½ miles of beach, grand hotels and a movie theater, built in 1936 to house the Mostra Festival.
San Michele
→ *Line n° 41/42, exit at Cimitero*
Famous for its pink walls, this island is the site of Venice's main cemetery.
Cimitero
→ *Tel. 041 528 95 18*
Tombs of Stravinsky, Ezra Pound, Diaghilev...
Murano
→ *Line n° 12, 13 and 41/42, exit at Faro*

The island of the master glassblowers.
Museo Vetrario
→ *Fondamenta Giustinian, 8*
Tel. 041 73 95 86
From antique glass to contemporary works.
Burano
→ *Line n° 12, exit at Burano*
The island of lacemakers.
Torcello
→ *Boat n° 12 (after Burano)*
A ghostly charm fills this almost deserted island, a former metropolis until supplanted by Venice.

ALTERNATIVE TRANSPORT

By gondola
Enjoy a romantic ride on the Lagoon's clear waters.
→ *Ente della Gondola*
Tel. 041 520 52 75 (res.)
Price 61 € (50 mins, day);
78 € (50 mins, 8pm–8am);
max 6 pers.
By rowing boat
Canottieri Diadora

Piazza San Marco / Castello (southwest)

The splendid buildings on Piazza San Marco, itself over a thousand years old, are true reminders of the political and cultural significance of Venice over the centuries. The stately processions and ducal enthronings may be a thing of the past, but Piazza San Marco, the 'Drawing Room of Europe' as Napoleon called it, still continues to draw millions of visitors each year from all over the world. To the east, via Riva degli Schiavoni, make your way into Castello, the largest of Venice's *sestieri* (districts), and discover its beautiful houses, palaces, churches, luxury boutiques and souvenir stalls.

GRAND CANAL RESTAURANT | CAFFÈ FLORIAN

RESTAURANTS

Le Bistrot de Venise (**A** A1)
→ San Marco,
Calle dei Fabbri, 4685
Tel. 041 523 66 51
Daily 9am–1am
This wine bar restaurant, decorated in wood and colored glass, has something of the atmosphere of a bistro in Paris' Montmartre. The cuisine, although Venetian, has a slight French accent too: home-made ravioli with herbs and *fromage frais*, sturgeons with wild artichokes and lemon sauce... Also readings, poetry evenings, concerts, art exhibitions and a piano. À la carte 26 €.

Trattoria do Forni (**A** B2)
→ San Marco, Calle Specchieri, 457 and 468
Tel. 041 523 21 48
Daily noon–3.30pm, 7pm–midnight
Close to Campo San Zulian, this is something of an institution:'Orient Express'-style woodwork and quality Venetian fare. Scallops with cep mushrooms, spaghetti with cockles, grilled fish, and wines from all over the world. A favorite with tourists and locals alike. À la carte 62 €.

Grand Canal Restaurant (**A** A3)
→ Hotel Monaco, San Marco
Calle Vallaresso, 1325
Tel. 041 520 02 11
Daily noon–3pm, 7.30–10.30pm
Dine on a terrace overlooking the Grand Canal and the church of La Salute. Top quality traditional and modern Italian cuisine such as crawfish salad with zucchini, salmon and swordfish tartare with peppers, *bigoli* (whole-meal spaghetti) *en sauce*, liver *à la Vénitienne*. Excellent wine list. À la carte 73 €.

Quadri (**A** A2)
→ San Marco,
Piazza San Marco, 120
Procuratie Vecchie
Tel. 041 528 92 99
Daily 12.15–2pm, 7.15–10.15pm.
Closed Mon in winter
From the dining room, well worthy of the Doges' Palace, there are unbeatable views of Piazza San Marco and the basilica. Elegant Venetian cuisine: saffron scallops, home-made pasta with crawfish and basil, pear, rocket and parmesan salad. Delicious desserts. Reservations essential. À la carte around 78 €.

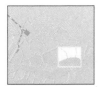

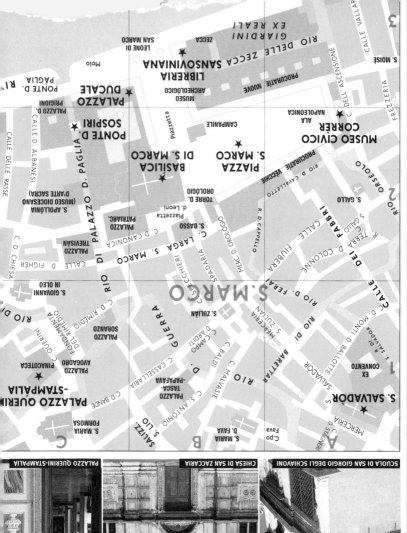

PALAZZO QUERINI-STAMPALIA

CHIESA DI SAN ZACCARIA

SCUOLA DI SAN GIORGIO DEGLI SCHIAVONI

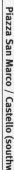

ÍSOLA DI MURANO

FOND. SERENELLA

RIO D. VETRAI

C. MIOTTI

CANALE DEI MARANI

CANALE DELLE NAVI

S. MICHELE

CIMITERO

ÍSOLA DI S. MICHELE

CANALE DELLE FONDAMENTA NUOVE

FONDAMENTA NUOVE

F

GESUITI

FONDAMENTA NUOVE

RIO D. S. CATERINA

RIO D. SS. APOSTOLI

RIO D. MENDICANTI

SS. GIOVANNI E PAOLO

SS. APÓSTOLI

S. MARIA D. MIRÁCOLI

S. FRANCESCO D. VIGNA

R. DI S. GIOV. LATERANO

S. MARIA FORMOSA

R. DI S. LORENZO

S. LORENZO

S. SALVADÓR

SCUOLA DI S. GIÓRGIO D. SCHIAVONI

DÁRSENA

CAN. DI P.TA NUOVA

ÍSOLA DI S. PIETRO

MERCERIE

R. DI S. SEVERO

R. DI S. LORENZO

TORRI D. ARESENALE

GRANDE

CAN. DI S. PIETRO

S MARCO

S. MARCO

LA PIETÀ

CASTELLO

CORDERÍE

C.o di S. PIETRO

CAN. DI QUINTAVALLE

P.za S. Marco

RIVA DEGLI SCHIAVONI

MUS. STORICO NAVALE

PAL. D. SPORT

D. TANA

A

PAL. DUCALE

VIA GARIBALDI

LA MARINARESSA

P.TA D. DOGANA

BACINO DI S. MARCO

RIVA D. 7 MARTIRI

R. DI S. GIUSEPPE

SECCO MARINA

CAN. DI GIARDINI

BIENNALE INTERNAZIONALE D'ARTE

RIVA D. PARTIGIANI

VIALE

STADIO S. ELENA

BACINO

S. GIÓRGIO MAGGIORE

CANALE DI S. MARCO

V.LE 4 NOVEMBRE

ÍSOLA DI S. ELENA

PIAVE

S. ELENA

CAN. DELLA GRAZIA

FOND. D. ZITELLE

ÍSOLA DI S. GIÓRGIO MAGGIORE

TEATRO VERDE

ZITELLE

V.LE VITT. VÉNETO

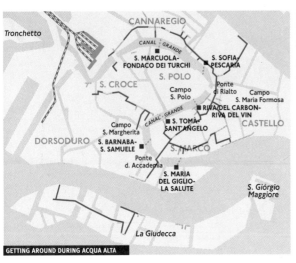

GETTING AROUND DURING ACQUA ALTA

'La vasca'
The evening stroll: groups of young people or families pass from one *campo* to the next, or walk along the Zattere, stopping for ice cream.

Evening
In the late evening the streets are empty. Nightowls head for the bars around Santa Margherita and on the Rialto or for the clubs on the Mestre.

Bacari
Nightlife in Venice is focused around bistros where the young (and less young) can meet and drink until 1–2am.

CHURCHES

Opening times
Usually 8am–12.30pm, 4–8pm

Information
→ *Chorus Associazione*
Tel. 041 275 04 62
For information on Venice's churches. Also helps in the preservation of churches by organizing a circuit that covers 13 among the most important examples of Venetian religious architecture.
Price 1.55 € per church;
Pass 7.75 € for circuit
email: chorus@tin.it
www.chorus-ve.org

Dress code
No shorts or short skirts.

CALENDAR OF EVENTS

February
Carnevale (carnival): the 10 days before Lent.

April 25
Festival of San Marco, the patron saint of the city, with gondola racing.

May
Su e zo per i ponti: bridge race; festival of the Ascension: procession and *vogalonga* (20-mile regatta Venice-Burano).

June-October
Biennale: international fair of either contemporary art (odd-numbered years) or architecture (even-numbered years).

July
Murano and Malamocco regattas; festival of the Redeemer (3rd Sat).

August
Festival of the Madonna at Pellestrina (1st week).

September
La Mostra: international film festival (last Sun. in Aug/1st week Sep); Regata Storica: gondola race and parade (1st Sun).

October
Sant'Erasmo regatta.

Venice marathon.

November 21
Festa della Salute.

USEFUL NUMBERS

Tourist office
→ *Azienda di Promozione Turistica (APT) San Marco, Calle dell'Ascensione, 71* (**A** A3) *Tel. 041 529 87 40*
There are three main kiosks in Venice.

Police
→ *Tel. 112 and 113*

Fire service
→ *Tel. 115*

Ambulance service
→ *Tel. 118*

Lost property
→ *AMAV. Tel. 041 521 70 11*

WWW.

→ *comune.venezia.it*
→ *turismovenezia.it*
The tourist office website.
→ *doge.it*
Information on Venice.
→ *venezia.net*

Revived in 1980, countless tourists from all over the world descend on the city in February for ten days (and nights) of utter mayhem.

Traditional carnival
Piazza San Marco: procession and festival (Sat); *Volo della Colombina* (Sun); huge masked ball (Fri).

Festivities
The atmosphere tends to be more spontaneous around the university and Campo Santa Margherita.

Getting around
Special police monitor the pedestrian traffic on the bridges.

What to eat
Carnival specialty: *fritole*, hot donuts with currants.

LIDO

ZATTERE

THE RIALTO MARKET

ACQUA ALTA

Between Nov and April, due to the combined effects of the wind and the strong tides, Venice is submerged at high tide (*acqua alta*). Follow the red routes shown on the map (right) and buy some wellingtons, perhaps at **Fratelli Regini** (**F** A4)
→ *Castello, Calle al Ponte di Sant'Antonio, 5615*
Tel. 041 520 43 47
Traghetti
To cross the Grand Canal, take a *traghetto*, one of the fleet of gondolas that make the crossing for as little as 0.45 €. The seven embarcation points are shown on the map (right).

main course.
Prices
Naturally prices tend to be higher in the more touristy areas. A charge for cover and bread (*pane e coperto*) is usually added to the cost of a main meal (around 1 € per person).
Classic
Ristoranti, pizzerie, pasticcerie (deli-cafés) and *tavole calde* (prepared hot food).
Osterie and bacari
Small, typically Italian eateries that are usually busy at lunchtime. When available, try some *cicchetti* (hot or cold snacks) at the bar before your main course.

SHOWS

Listings and information on concerts, shows, cinema, events
Ospite di Venezia
→ *Monthly in winter, weekly in summer. Free from tourist*

offices and some hotels. Show listings in Italian and English.
Venezia News
→ *Monthly, free (available from cafés)*
Comprehensive listings in Italian and English (theater, classical concerts, rock, film, restaurants, etc.).
Reservations
Cassa di Risparmio (**B** F1)
→ *San Marco, Campo San Luca, 4216 Tel. 041 521 0161*
Theater, concert and opera tickets.
Classical concerts
Basilica dei Frari (**D** B4)
→ *San Polo, Campo dei Frari*
Tel. 041 522 26 37
The best of Venetian religious music.
Santa Maria della Pietà
(**A** E2)
→ *Castello, Riva degli Schiavoni*
Tel. 041 523 10 96
Major concerts of baroque music held in a church where Antonio Vivaldi was

once choirmaster.
Scuola Grande di San Rocco
(**D** A4)
→*San Polo, Campo San Rocco*
Tel. 041 962 999
Baroque music and orchestras from all over the world.
Opera
PalaFenice
→ *Tronchetto island*
Tel. 041 786 520
www.teatrolafenice.it
A marquee seating up to 1,200; currently home to La Fenice productions while its main house is being rebuilt.
Theaters
Teatro Goldoni (**D** E4)
→ *San Marco, Corte del Teatro 4650 / B*
Tel. 041 520 54 22
Home to the Teatro Stabile del Veneto.
Teatro a l'Avogaria (**C** E3)
→ *Dorsoduro, Calle Lunga San Barnaba, 1607*
Tel. 041 520 92 70
Renaissance works by the Giovanni Poli company.

MUSEUMS

Opening times
Very variable. In general, later closing times in high season (April-Sep).
Reduced rates
These vary depending on the museum. In general they apply to students 18–25 years and the over-60s.
Free entry
Free entry to the Diocesanodi Arte Sacra and Archeologico museums, and to Goldoni's house.
Municipal museums
There is an entrance fee for most of Venice's major municipal museums.
→ *From 3.10 € to 6.20 €*
Biglietto cumulativo
→ *9.30 €*
Allows group entry to the Palazzi Ducale and Mocenigo, Museo Correr, Museo dell'Arte Vetrario and Scuola di Merletti.

PALAZZO
GIUSTINIÀN

ESSO

CAPITANERIA
DI PORTO

FOND. D. FARINE

S. MARCO

BACINO DI S. MARCO

4

PUNTA
DELLA DOGANA

DOGANA
DA MAR

A   B   C

LIBRERIA SANSOVINIANA

PIAZZA SAN MARCO

★ **Scuola di San Giorgio
degli Schiavoni** (**A** F1)
→ *Castello, Calle dei Furlani,
3259/A Tel. 041 522 88 28*
Summer: *Tue–Sat 9.30am–
12.30pm, 3.30–6.30pm;
Sun 9.30am–12.30pm*
Winter: *Mon-Sat 10am–noon,
3–6pm; Sun 10am–12.30pm*
In 1502 the influential
Dalmatian *scuola* commis-
sioned Carpaccio to paint
these nine fabulous
canvases depicting scenes
of the protector saints, the
most famous of which is
St George and the Dragon.
★ **Chiesa
di San Zaccaria** (**A** D2)
→ *Castello, Campo San
Zaccaria, 5252
Tel. 041 522 12 57*

*Mon-Sat 10am–noon,
4–6pm; Sun 4–6pm*
Altarpiece by Bellini,
paintings by Vivarini and
Alemagna... the incredible
richness of the interior
of this church, a former
14th-century sanctuary, is
thanks to the control of
the nearby convent whose
nuns all came from rich and
powerful Venetian families.
★ **Palazzo Querini-
Stampalia** (**A** C1)
→ *Castello, Campiello
Querini Stampalia, 4778
Tel. 041 271 14 11
Daily 10am–1pm, 3–6pm
(10pm Fri and Sat)*
This Renaissance palace,
once owned by the Querini
family, was donated to

the city in 1868 by the last
of that line. The garden
has been immaculately
restored, as was the
building itself, by Carlo
Scarpa in 1960. Don't
miss the rich collection of
paintings in the foundation
art gallery, including the
series of small paintings
of 18th-century Venice by
Pietro Longhi.
★ **Palazzo Ducale /
Doges' Palace** (**A** C3)
→ *Piazzetta San Marco
Tel. 041 522 49 51
April-Oct: daily 9am–5.30pm
Nov-Mar: daily 9am–3.30pm*
Emblem of the Republic,
the Doges' Palace is a
masterpiece of Gothic
architecture (14th–15th

centuries). In an unusual
subversion of equilibrium,
the airily light galleries and
arcades appear to support
a heavy upper structure.
This former seat of political
and legal affairs boasts
a courtyard and lovely
apartments filled with
canvases by Old Masters
(Tintoretto, Palma the
Younger, Veronese...)
depicting the city's great
historical events.
★ **Ponte dei Sospiri /
Bridge of Sighs** (**A** C2)
→ *Piazzetta San Marco*
Far from having a romantic
origin, the 'sighs' were
those of convicts crossing
from the law courts to the
dungeons, whose last

ARRY'S BAR

VENETIA STUDIUM

VENINI

PUBS, CAFÉS, WINE BARS

Devil's Forest Pub (A A1)
→ San Marco,
Calle degli Stagneri, 5185
Tel. 041 52 00 623
Daily 10am–1am
An Irish-style pub in the heart of the city of the Doges. Wide choice of Irish beers; pop music and boisterous darts tournaments. Draught beer 1.80 €–4.70 €. Snacks only.

Caffè Florian (A A3)
→ San Marco,
Piazza San Marco, 56–59
Procuratie Nuove
Tel. 041 528 53 38
Daily 9.30am–midnight
Closed 10 days before Christmas and 10 days at the beginning of Jan.
This historic café has been tucked away under the arcades of Piazza San Marco since 1720. To Balzac Florian was 'a reading room, a theater foyer, a confessional, a stock exchange and a club.' It is sumptuous and expensive, but unmissable. At least come here for a coffee (6.50 € but served on a silver tray!) and enjoy the 18th-century setting: gilding, woodwork and beautiful old mirrors. In summer:

classical concerts on the terrace.

Gran Caffè Quadri (A A2)
→ San Marco,
Piazza San Marco, 120
Procuratie Vecchie
Tel. 041 522 21 05
Daily 9am–midnight
Closed Mon in winter
Equally prestigious as its neighbor Florian, even if it is not so well known internationally. Yellow wall-paper, baroque furniture, upholstered armchairs... Stunning terrace overlooking the basilica. Coffee 3.85 €.

Harry's Bar (A A3)
→ San Marco,
Calle Vallaresso, 1323
Tel. 041 528 57 77
Daily 10.30am–11pm
Hemingway created his explosive cocktail here: 15 parts gin to 1 part vermouth! Many other celebrities (Onassis, Woody Allen) have also succumbed to Harry's old-fashioned charm. House cocktail: Bellini (prosecco and peach liquor). Prices are lower if you sit at the bar (where they also serve food). Coffee 2.50 €.

Gran Caffè Lavena (A B2)
→ San Marco,
Piazza San Marco, 133-134
Tel. 041 522 40 70
Daily 9.30am–11.30pm

Closed Tue in winter
Excellent pastries and the best espresso in town. Sit inside, at the bar, or outside on the terrace (additional charge). Coffee 3.60 €.

Moscacieka (A A2)
→ San Marco,
Calle dei Fabbri, 4717
Tel. 041 520 80 85
Mon-Sat 9am–1pm
Pop music and a young, relaxed atmosphere. Fight your way through the crowd to the lovely blue-mosaic bar. For a quieter atmosphere, there are little tables at the rear. Cocktails 4.15 €, sandwiches 2 €–3.10 €.

SHOPPING

Paola e Mario Bevilacqua (A C2)
→ San Marco, Fondamenta Canonica (al ponte), 337/B
Tel. 041 522 95 81
Daily 10am–7pm
Tapestries, cushions, silks and fabrics embroidered here since the 17th century in the true Venetian tradition. Prices start at 130 € for a small handbag.

Jesurum (A A3)
→ San Marco,
Piazza San Marco, 60-61
Tel. 041 522 98 64
Mon-Sat 9.30am–7.30pm,
Sun 10am–1pm, 2–7pm

An institution since 1870. Household linen in elegant, high-quality Venetian fabrics.

Venetia Studium (A A1)
→ San Marco, Merceria 723
Tel. 041 522 98 59
Mon-Sat 9.30am–8pm,
Sun 10.30am–7.30pm
Studio selling silks, and renowned for its famous pleated 'Fortuny' silk. Velvet and crêpe, capes, purses, scarves and lampshades. Expensive, but superb.

Venini (A B2)
→ San Marco,
Piazzetta dei Leoni, 314
Tel. 041 522 40 45
Summer Mon-Sat 10am–7.30pm/Winter Tue-Sat 10am-12.30pm, 3.30-7.30pm
Stunning contemporary creations in Murano blownglass. Lamps, chandeliers and vases in avant-garde designs and bright colors. Original designs made to order.

Bruno Magli (A A3)
→ San Marco, Calle dell' Ascensione, 1302
Tel. 041 522 72 10
Daily 10am–7pm
Very elegant shoes for men and women: classics in winter, more decorative designs in summer (with pearls, raffia, etc). Also carries a range of lovely real-leather purses.

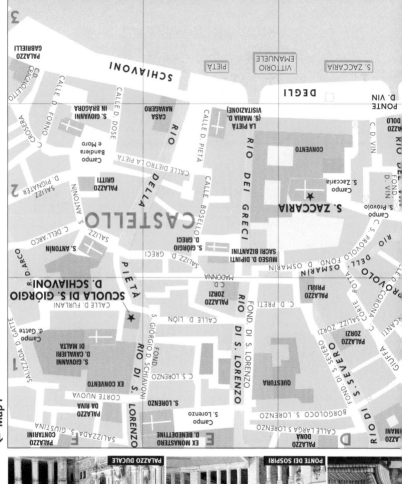

PALAZZO DUCALE

PONTE DEI SOSPIRI

Map F

3

PALAZZO GABRIELLI

C. GRASSIOLETTO

CALLE D. FORNO

C. CROSERA

SALIZZ. D. PIGNATER

SCHIAVONI

VITTORIO EMANUELE

PIETÀ

S. ZACCARIA

DEGLI

PONTE D. VIN

C. D. VIN
DOLO
OZZA
RIO DEL

S. GIOVANNI IN BRAGORA

CALLE D. DOSE

CASA NAVAGERO

RIO D. PIETÀ

CALLE DIETRO LA PIETÀ

LA PIETÀ (S. MARIA D. VISITAZIONE)

CONVENTO

Campo Bandiera e Moro

CALLE DELLA PIETÀ

CALLE BOSELLO

RIO DEI GRECI

S. Zaccaria

Campo S. Provolo

FOND. D. VIN

PALAZZO GRITTI

S. ANTONIN

C. DELL'ARCO

S. ANTONIN

SALIZZ. D. GRECI

S. GIORGIO D. GRECI

MUSEO D. DIPINTI SACRI BIZANTINI

S. ZACCARIA

Campo S. Provolo

RIO DELL'OSMARIN

FOND. D. OSMARIN

RIO DI SAN LORENZO

CASTELLO

R. D. ARCO

C.D. MADONNA

SALIZZ. D. GRECI

PIETÀ

C.D.

SCUOLA DI S. GIORGIO D. SCHIAVONI

CALLE D. FURLANI

S. GIORGIO D. SCHIAVONI

FOND. D. GATTE

Campo d. Gatte

SALIZZADA D. GATTE

PALAZZO PRIULI

RIO DI S. LORENZO

PALAZZO ZORZI

C.D. PRETI

FOND. DI S. SEVERO

CORTE ROTTA

C. CORONA

PALAZZO ZORZI

GIUFFA

RIO DI S. SEVERO

BORGOLOCO S. LORENZO

QUESTURA

S. GIOVANNI D. CAVALIERI DI MALTA

EX CONVENTO

CORTE NUOVA

PALAZZO DA RIVA

S. LORENZO

Campo S. Lorenzo

CALLE D. LION

FOND. DI S. LORENZO

C. S. LORENZO

PALAZZO CONTARINI

SALIZZADA S. GIUSTINA

EX MONASTERO D. BENEDETTINE

CALLE LARGA S. LORENZO

PALAZZO DONÀ

RIO DI S. MANI OZZA

1

D

ANALE DI S. MARCO

4

0   50   100 m
110 yards

D   E   F

USEO CIVICO CORRER

BASILICA DI SAN MARCO

CHIESA DI SAN SALVADOR

glimpse of freedom was the view from this bridge. Tours of the Doge's Palace include visits to the prison, a major attraction being the cell that Casanova is said to have escaped from in 1755.

★ **Libreria Sansoviniana** (**A** B3)

→ *Piazzetta San Marco, 13*
Tel. 041 520 87 88
Daily 9am–7pm
The 21 arches of this façade mirror those of the Doges' Palace opposite. Designed in 1537 by Sansovino, this is Venice's most important library, housing rarities such as a Grimiani bible with Flemish illuminations and a 1487 edition of Dante's *Divine*

Comedy, displayed beneath frescoes by Titian, Veronese and Tintoretto.

★ **Piazza San Marco** (**A** B2)
The theatrical grandeur of Venice's most spectacular monuments dominates this breathtaking piazza. Usually quiet in the early hours and frequently flooded at *acqua alta* (high tide). Superb views from the *campanile*.

★ **Museo Civico Correr** (**A** A2)

→ *Piazza San Marco, 52*
Tel. 041 522 56 25
April-Oct: daily 9am–7pm
Nov-March: daily 9am–5pm
Unmissable for its 13th–16th-century Venetian

painting and for its depiction of the city's history. Lodged in the Procuratie Nuove, this is Venice's loveliest museum and displays statues, pictures, costumes, weapons...

★ **Basilica di San Marco** (**A** B2)

→ *Piazza San Marco, 30124*
Tel. 041 522 56 97
Mon-Sat 9.45am–5pm;
Sun 2–5pm
Stunning Byzantine-style basilica, heavily influenced by centuries of trade with the East. Inspired by Istanbul's St Sophia, the 5 domes were added in 1094, changing the look of the basilica, originally built to house St Mark's

remains, (brought from Alexandria in 829). Luxurious and elaborate décor: 40,000 sq. ft of mosaics, marble tiling, gilding – including the famous Pala d'Oro (14th century), a golden altar-piece inlaid with precious gems and enamel.

★ **Chiesa di San Salvador** (**A** A1)

→ *San Marco,*
Campo San Salvador
Tel. 041 523 67 17
Daily 9am–noon, 3.30–7pm
Very elegant Tuscan church topped with 3 Byzantine-style domes like those of San Marco. Don't miss Titian's *Annunciation*. (1566).

PALAZZO VENIER DEI LEONI

CHIESA DI SANTA MARIA DELLA SALUTE

DOGANA DA MAR

★ Palazzo Contarini del Bovolo (B E1)

→ San Marco,
Corte del Bovolo, 4299
Tel. 041 270 24 64
April-Oct: daily 10am-5.30pm
The famous spiral staircase is a feat of architectural brilliance. Added on to the main building in c. 1499, it links the loggias to the palace itself.

★ Chiesa di San Moisè

→ San Marco (B F2)
Campo San Moisè, 1390
Tel. 041 528 58 40 Daily
3.30–6.30pm (6pm in winter)
The elaborate decoration (statues, bas reliefs) renders this church one of the most controversial in

Venice: a baroque master-piece to some, over-the-top to others. Don't miss La Lavanda dei Piedi by Tintoretto, or the Last Supper, attributed to Palma the Younger.

★ Palazzo Grassi

→ San Marco, Campo di San Samuele, 3231
Tel. 041 523 16 80
Daily 9/10am–7pm
(depending on exhibitions)
One of the most active cultural centers in the world with exhibitions ranging from 'the Phoenicians' to 'Andy Warhol'. Based in one of the last palaces to be built under La Serenissima (1749), it was renovated in

1984 in a masterly way by Gae Aulenti (architect for Paris' Orsay Museum) and Antonio Foscari.

★ Palazzo Pisani (B C2)

→ San Marco,
Campiello Pisani, 2810
Tel. 041 522 56 04
Loggias, staircases, labyrinthine courtyards, porticos, this is an exceptional example of Venetian Gothic design. Open-air operas and ballets in summer on the campo. Magnificent flight of steps right next to the canal.

★ Gallerie dell'Accademia (B B3)

→ Dorsoduro, Campo della Carità, 1050

Tel. 041 522 22 47
Mon 8.15am–2pm;
Tue-Sat 8.15am–7pm
Exceptional collection of Venetian 14th–18th century paintings from Bellini, Lotto and Tintoretto to Tiepolo. Founded in 1807, the galleries also house the Academy of Fine Arts.

★ Palazzo Venièr dei Leoni (B D3)

→ Dorsoduro,
Calle San Cristoforo, 701
Tel. 041 520 62 88
Wed-Mon 11am–10pm (6pm in winter)
The Palazzo Venier houses one of the world's most important modern art collections, assembled by

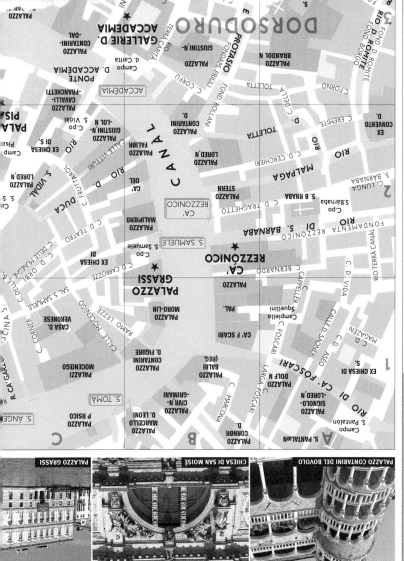

DORSODURO

GALLERIE D. ACCADEMIA

PALAZZO CONTARINI-DAL

PONTE D. ACCADEMIA

PALAZZO CAVALLI-FRANCHETTI

ACCADEMIA

Campo d. Carità

PALA PISA

C.po S. Vidal

PALAZZO PROTASIO

FONDAM. PRIULI

C. CORFU

PALAZZO CONTARINI D.

C. DELLA TOLETTA

C.FORNO

EX CHIESA DI S.

PALAZZO LORED. N

S. VIDAL

RIO D.

CALLE VITTURI

C. FRUTTAROL

PALAZZO GIUSTINI-N.-LOL N

CANAL

PALAZZO LOREDAN

PALAZZO FALIER

TOLETTA

C. D. CERCHIERI

RIO

EX CONVENTO D.

C. CREMITE

RIO

DEL

CA'

PALAZZO STERN

MALPAGA

C.LUNGA S. BARNABA

C.po S.Barnaba

C.D. TRAGHETTO

S. B RNABA

FONDAMENTA REZZONICO

RIO TERRÀ CANAL

C. D. TEATRO

C. D. BATTELLE

C.D. ORBI

SAL. S. SAMUELE

C.po S. Samuele

PALAZZO MALIPIERO

S. SAMUELE

EX CHIESA DI

C.po S.Samuele

CA' REZZONICO

RIO DI S. BARNABA

C. BERNARDO

CAPPELLER

C. D. VIDA

C.D. MAGAZEN

C. GARZOZE

PALAZZO GRASSI

PALAZZO MORO-LIN

PALAZZO

C. BERNARDO

Campiello Squellini

C. D. SIGNERI

C.D. ASÈO

CALLE D. SAONERI

RIO TERRÀ CANAL

R. CA' GARZ

CASA D. CORNER

C. CORNER

C. VERONESE

RAMO LEZZE

CALLE MOCENIGO

PALAZZI MOCENIGO

CA' F SCARI

PAL.

CALLE LARGA FOSCARI

C. D. ASÈO

S. ANGE

P PSICO

PALAZZO

PALAZZO MARCELLO D. LEONI

S. TOMA

PALAZZO CONTARINI D. FIGURE

CIVR N.-GRIMANI

PALAZZO BALBI (REG.)

C. F SCARI

C. MARCONA

PALAZZO DOLF N

LARGA C. FOSCARI

EX CHIESA DI

CALLE LARGA FOSCARI

RIO DI CA' FOSCARI

PALAZZO SIGNOLO-LORED. N

C

PALAZZO CORNER D.

S. PANTAL∂N

Campo S. Pantalon

Located at the final curve of the Grand Canal, the district of San Marco is the heart of aristocratic Venice, filled with grand hotels, banks, and luxury and antique shops. Take the elegant Campo Santo Stefano to the Accademia bridge, the only vaulted wooden bridge in Venice, and cross over to the Dorsoduro district. The Grand Canal unfolds toward the east, where three of the city's largest museums reside, and ends at the headland of La Salute and the former customs houses. The streets grow wider as you approach the Zàttere, where Venetians like to stroll and take in the panoramic views of the Giudecca and San Giorgio Maggiore islands.

DA CARLA

AL BACARETO

RESTAURANTS

Osteria Ai Assassini (**B** E1)
➜ San Marco, Rio Terrà dei Assassini, 3695
Tel. 041 528 79 86
Mon-Sat 11.30am–3pm, 6.30pm–midnight
Closed for 15 days in Aug.
A popular hang-out for students and lecturers at Venice University. Home-made pasta, soup, fish (Fri. and Sat.) and daily specials. Attractive rustic-style dining room and a small terrace on the street. À la carte 18 €.

Da Carla (**B** F2)
➜ San Marco, Corte Contarina, 1535
Tel. 041 523 78 55
Mon-Sat 7.30am–10pm
A few paces from Piazza San Marco, a traditional osteria with a pretty painted sign hanging outside. Good choice of salads, home-made pasta, soups. Specialties: cuttlefish, polenta and fried fish. Italian wine served in pitchers. Terrace. À la carte 21 €.

Trattoria da Fiore (**B** C1)
➜ San Marco, Calle delle Botteghe, 3461
Tel. 041 523 53 10
Wed-Mon noon–3pm, 7–10pm

Risottos, sepie (cuttlefish) and polenta, deep-fried calamari, fish, antipasti buffet... Classic Venetian cooking served in an elegant setting. The bar opens onto the street and serves a range of ciccheti (snacks) and wine by the glass. À la carte 36 €.

Al Bacareto (**B** C1)
➜ San Marco, Calle delle Botteghe, 3447
Tel. 041 528 93 36
Mon-Fri 7.30am–midnight; Sat 7.30am–4pm.
Closed Aug.
This family-run trattoria has specialized in fresh pasta and fish dishes since the 19th century: cod with polenta, spaghetti with cuttlefish or cep mushrooms. Delicious dolce (desserts) including amoretto (mascarpone mousse with almond liquor). Pleasant terrace, very lively in summer. À la carte 31 €.

BAKERIES, ICE CREAM PARLORS

Gelateria Nico (**B** D4)
➜ Dorsoduro, Fondamenta Zàttere allo Spirito Santo, 922
Tel. 041 522 52 93
Summer: daily 7.30am–

To the west of the Dorsoduro, the peaceful quaysides are a wonderful excuse for a quiet walk along the Giudecca canal, with the breeze sweeping in from the Lagoon. On the Squero di San Trovaso, an image of times past, craftspeople carry out extraordinarily detailed repair work on the gondolas. Toward the north, taking the *rii* of San Nicolo and Angelo Raffaele, you reach Campo Santa Margherita. Here you will find a completely different side of Venice: it is a student area with colorful houses, shady terraces and countless cafés on the lively Campo – perfect for a light lunch or a relaxed pre-dinner drink.

AL BOTTEGON RANDON

RESTAURANTS

Al Bottegon (**C** F4)
→ *Dorsoduro,
Fondamenta Nani, 992*
Tel. 041 523 00 34
*Mon-Sat 8am–2.30pm,
3.30–8.30pm;
Sun 10am–1pm
Closed last week in Aug*
Traditional little *osteria* which has been in the same family for three generations. Students and teachers come here for a glass of wine and enormous *panini* (cheese, Parma ham, mortadella, rocket, *bressaola*).
À la carte 13 €.

Ai Sportivi (**C** E2)
→ *Dorsoduro,
Campo Santa Margherita,
3052*
Tel. 041 521 15 98
*Daily 11.30am–3pm,
7–11.30pm*
The best pizzas in town, all topped with the very flavorsome *mozzarella di bufala*. The house special is the *paradiso* (tomato, *bressaola* and *grana*). Home-made pasta, meat dishes and a variety of salads. Pizzas from 4.20 € to 8.30 €.

Osteria da Toni (**C** C3)
→ *Dorsoduro,
Fondamenta San Basilio,
1642*

Tel. 041 528 68 99
*Tue-Sun 7am–8pm
Closed Aug 15 – 1st week
of Sep*
In the kitchen, Ciugola cooks delicious traditional Italian fare with whatever fresh produce she's just been buying from the market. Baked lasagne, calves liver with onions, braised cuttlefish are among the dishes on offer. Also a wide choice of sandwiches and *panini*.
À la carte 13 €–26 €.

Randon (**C** F2)
→ *Dorsoduro,
Campo San Barnaba, 2852*
Tel. 041 522 44 10
*Tue-Sat 11am–3pm,
6–10pm; Mon 4–10pm*
Wooden décor with beams and pretty tiling, this bar-restaurant on the Campo San Barnaba has a quiet atmosphere. Local dishes (home-made pasta, lasagne, veal escalope in white wine, cheeses). Excellent wine list. À la carte 24 €.

PASTRY SHOPS

Tonolo (**C** F1)
→ *Dorsoduro,
Crosera San Pantalon, 3764*
Tel. 041 523 72 09
Tue-Sun 7.45am–9pm
People from all over the

FOND. DEI BARI

3

FRATI
Camp.
S. Sebastiano
C.po Angelo
Raffaele
LARDONI

ANGELO RAFFAELE

S. NICOLO D. MENDICOLI

RIO DI S. NICOLO
FOND. DI S. NICOLO

R. D. ANGELO RAFFAELE
FOND. S. SEBASTIANO
FOND. S. ANGELO RAFFAELE

FONDAMENTA BRIAT

FONDAMENTA ARIANI

PALAZZO ARIANI

FOND. BARBARIGO
FOND. DI PESCHERIA
FOND. DI LIZZA

Campo
S. Nicolo

FOND. DI. TRON
RIELO

RIO DI. TERESE

CALLE DE GUARDIANI

C.TE MAZOR

FOND. D. ARZERE
FOND. D. ARZERE

FOND. D. TERESE

S.

C. NOVA DELLE TERESE

D

2

RIO TERRA D. SECCHI

RIO DELL'ARZERE

C. DEL CRISTO

C. DELL'OLIO

FOND. DI FONTEGHERI

FONDAMENTA MALCANTON
FONDAMENTA CERERI

RIO DEL

C. VIOTTI

FOND. DI MADONNA

C. D. MADONNA

RIO DELL

RIO DI S. M. MAGGIORE
FONDAMENTA DELLE PROCURATIE

FOND. DI S. M. MAGGIORE

RIZZI

FOND.
CAZZIOLA

RIO DELLA CAZZIOLA

RIO TERRA DEI PENSIERI

EX CHIESA DI S. M. MAGGIORE

CANALE DI S. M. MAGGIORE

C

1

A

CHIESA DI SAN BARNABA

EX CHIESA DI SAN TROVASO | **CHIESA DI SAN TROVASO**

SQUERO DI SAN TROVASO

★ D. DOGANA

FONDAM. DOGANA ALLA SALUTE

Campo d. Salute

★ S. MARIA D. SALUTE

DOGANA DA MAR

SEMIN RIO PATRIARCALE

R. D. SALUTE

CALLE D. SOLERO

R. TERRÀ D. CATECÙMENI

EX OSPŒZIO

RIO TERRÀ AI SALONI

FOND. DELLA FORNACE

SALONI EX MAGAZZINI D. SALE

FOND. DELLA SALE

FONDAM. ZÀTTERE AI SALONI

CANALE DELLA GIUDECCA

SANTO

D   FONDAM. ZÀTTERE AI SALONI   E   F

4

0   50   100 m

I GESUATI   CA'REZZONICO

Peggy Guggenheim. Works by Dali, Picasso, Klee, Miró, Calder, Kandinsky and Bacon fill the unfinished Venièr building with all its 18th-century eccentricities. Lions were once chained in the courtyard, giving it the name of 'dei Leoni'.

★ Chiesa di Santa Maria della Salute (B E3)
→ Dorsoduro 1, Campo della Salute   Tel. 041 522 55 58
Daily 9am–noon, 3–5.30pm (5pm in winter)
At the mouth of the Grand Canal stands the most harmonious example of Venetian baroque architecture. Two majestic domes, flanked by campaniles in

Istrian stone, dominate their more modest surroundings. On Nov. 21 the Festa della Saluta takes place in homage to the Virgin for bringing an end to the plague epidemic of 1630.

★ Dogana da Mar (B F3)
→ Dorsoduro, Fondamenta della Dogana
Just where the Dorsoduro juts out into the Lagoon is the customs house, with excellent views of San Marco and the islands of San Giorgio and Guidecca. Set up in the 15th century to inspect ships, it is topped by a famous statue of 'Fortuna' perched on a golden globe, symbol of

the powerful Serenissima. The warehouses are currently being renovated.

★ I Gesuati (B B4)
→ Dorsoduro, Zattere ai Gesuati   Tel. 041 523 06 25
Mon-Sat 9am–6pm; Sun 1–6pm
One of the loveliest Rococo interiors in Venice. Stunning ceiling frescoes by Tiepolo (1737–9): Institution of the Rosary, The Glory of St Dominic. The Dominicans are responsible for the Palladian-inspired façade (Corinthian columns and pediment) built between 1724 and 1736. After the dissolution of the Jesuits

Order in 1668, it was dedicated to hospital service.

★ Ca' Rezzonico (B B2)
→ Dorsoduro 3136, Fondamenta Rezzonico
Tel. 041 241 01 00
Monumental palace (1667–1758) richly furnished, with frescoes by Tiepolo – amongst which his lovely Nuptial Allegory. Decorative art collections from the Settecento, the golden age of the republic: furniture (Andrea Brustolon) glass (ciocche, bouquet-shaped chandeliers), porcelain and tapestries. One room is dedicated to work by Longhi, another to portrait artist Rosalba Carriera.

BANCHINA DEL PORTO COMMERCIALE

CORD.

S. SEBASTI
EX

SALIZZ. S. BASÉGIO

BASILIO
BASÉGIO

STAZIONE
MARITTIMA

BANCHINA DI S. BASÉGIO

C.p
S. Bas

PALAZ
MOLI

S. BASÍLIO

CANALE DELLA GIUD

4

0   50   100 m
110 yards

A   B   C

CHIESA DELL'ANGELO RAFFAELE

CHIESA DI SAN NICOLÒ DEI MENDICOLI

CHIESA DEI CARMINI

★ Chiesa di San Barnaba (C F2)

➜ *Dorsoduro, Campo San Barnaba. Open for exhibitions Wed-Mon 10am–6pm*
The bell tower was built in the 11th century, an unusual conical spire added in the 1300s. The *campo*, a rectangle demarcated by the church at one end and the *rio* (canal) at the other, is a typical layout for the oldest of the *campi*. Close by is the Ponte dei Pugni, where the Castellani and the Nicolotti, rival clans, would meet to fist-fight until the 18th century, egged on by crowds of onlookers. Sculpted footprints show the position of the fighters.

★ Chiesa di San Trovaso (C F4)

➜ *Dorsoduro, Campo San Trovaso, 1098 Mon-Sat 8am–11am, 3–6pm*
It bears two identical, classical façades! Standing at the boundary of the parishes of two enemy clans, two entrances were essential. In the church, look for a fine Renaissance bas-relief (angels bearing the symbols of Christ's Passion), canvases by Tintoretto, and a *St Chrysogonus Mounted on a Horse* by Giambono (15th century).

★ Squero di San Trovaso (C F4)

➜ *Dorsoduro, Campo San Trovaso, 1097 (private)*
The *squero* (boatyard) has been active since the 1600s, and is now one of the last remaining gondola workshops in the city. Here they make, repair, clean and varnish the gondolas. The surprising chalet-like buildings are reminiscent of those of the Cadore, the area where many local crafts people originated from.

★ Zàttere (C DE4)

➜ *Dorsoduro, Canale della Giudecca*
Venetians like to take a stroll here. In 1640 the *fondamenta* (broad paved quaysides built in 1516) was designated as a landing point for lumber, delivered by flotation (*záttera*). The activity provided by the unloading of the rafts has been replaced by cafés and ice-cream sellers. Fabulous views of the Giudecca.

★ Chiesa di San Sebastiano (C C3)

➜ *Dorsoduro, Campo San Sebastiano Tel. 041 275 04 62 Mon-Sat 10am–5pm*
A series of dazzlingly colored paintings by Veronese, hidden away behind a modest façade. On the sacristy ceiling is his *Crowning of the Virgin* (1555), one of the first works he was commissioned to do. Until 1565 Veronese

C

GELATERIA NICO

AL VOLTO

ROLANDO SEGALIN

11.30pm / Winter: Mon-Wed, Fri-Sat 7am–10pm; Sun 7.30am–10pm
Try the celebrated *gianduitto* (creamy ice cream with chocolate, hazelnuts and whipped cream). Magnificent raised terrace opposite the Giudecca.
Ice cream 3.60 €–6 €.

Pasticceria Marchini (**B** D2)
→ *San Marco,*
Calle Zaguri, 2769
Tel. 041 522 91 09
Mon, Wed-Sun 8.30am–8.30pm
Endless variety of Venetian cookies, chocolates and candies in all sorts of colors and flavors. Specialty: *Torta del Doge*, a sweet almond pie.

CAFÉS, WINE BARS

Caffè di Torino (**B** F1)
→ *San Marco,*
Campo San Luca, 4591
Tel. 041 522 39 14
Mon-Sat 7.30am–7.30pm, 10pm–2am
By day a busy café, by night a lively bar; this is a great place to meet friends for a glass of wine, a beer or a spritzer.

Internet Café (**B** D2)
→ *San Marco,*
Campo Santo Stefano, 2967

and 2958
Tel. 041 277 11 90
Daily 9am–2am
The cheapest of the many cybercafés which now populate the city. Reduced-rate international calls and furious online games events on Sat. evenings.

Al Volto (**B** E1)
→ *San Marco,*
Calle Cavalli, 4081
Tel. 041 522 89 45
Mon-Sat 10am–2.30pm, 5–10.30pm
Welcoming wine specialist situated in a quiet backstreet overlooking the Grand Canal. The ceiling is plastered with Italian wine-bottle labels. Various *ciccheti* (snacks) are available, along with draught beer and wine by the glass or bottle (from 31€ to 310€).

Vino Vino (**B** E2)
→ *San Marco,*
Calle delle Veste, 2007/A
Tel. 041 241 76 88
Wed-Mon 10.30am–midnight (1am on Sat)
Attractive little wine bar, a particular favorite with the student community. Italian and international vintages by the glass or the bottle: Mionetto Vivo (3.10 €), Azelia Bardo 1995 (34 €). Also offers a

limited menu of hot and cold dishes.

SHOPPING

Arras (**B** A1)
→ *Dorsoduro,*
Campiello Squellini, 3234
Tel. 041 522 64 60
Mon-Sat 9am–1pm,
3.30–7.30pm.
Closed for 2 weeks in Aug.
Pants, shirts, vest-tops... all hand made, in silk, linen or cotton. Tapestries and fabrics made to order by the excellent Venetian co-operative Fiorita Tapis.

Nalesso (**B** D1)
→ *San Marco,*
Calle Spezier, 2765
Tel. 041 520 33 29
Mon-Sat 9.30am–12.30pm,
3.30–7.30pm
The biggest classical music shop in Venice. Scores, instruments, Venetian music and up-to-date classical concert information and listings.

Antichitá Zaggia (**B** A2)
→ *Dorsoduro,*
Calle della Toletta, 1195
Tel. 041 522 31 59
Mon-Sat 9am–1pm, 3.30–7.30pm. Closed in July.
A quaint little shop, selling a wide range of jewelry (bracelets, earrings, necklaces), and accessories made

from real old-pearl of Murano blown glass.

Rolando Segalin (**B** F1)
→ *San Marco,*
Calle dei Fuseri, 4365
Tel. 041 522 21 15
Mon-Fri 9am–noon, 3.30–7pm; Sat 9am–noon.
Closed for 2 weeks in Aug.
In this studio, which first opened in 1932, Rolando Segalin creates the most extravagant shoes in Venice: Casanova shoes, slippers made in mock zebra skin, derbys, eccentric carnival shoes. Also does repairs and will take on original designs on request.

Alberto Valese-Ebrû (**B** D2)
→ *San Marco,*
Campo Santo Stefano, 3471
Tel. 041 523 88 30
Mon-Sat 10am-7pm; Sun 11am–6pm. Closed Sun in Aug. and 2 weeks in Aug.
One of the best paper-makers in Venice: marbled paper with various motifs (flowers, animals) used for diaries, photo albums, note-books, etc. The shop also sells articles made from painted or printed silk, thus those who really care for detail will be able to buy a necktie that matches their organiser.

city frequent this patisserie, first opened in 1866. Specialties: *focaccia* (soft bread with almonds), *nonna pina* (small, flavored, cookies) and other delicious goodies. At the counter, excellent cappuccino.

CAFÉS, CONCERTS

Codroma (C C2)
→ *Dorsoduro,*
Fondamenta del Soccorso,
2540
Tel. 041 524 67 89
Mon-Fri 8am–10pm;
Sun 9am–1.30pm, 4–11pm
Located at the foot of a bridge, this pretty *osteria* is wickedly retro in style and harbors a rather young clientele. Piano-bar on Thu. In winter, live rock and jazz concerts on Tue. from 9pm. Beer 1.60 € – 2.60 €.
Café Blue (C F1)
→ *Dorsoduro,*
Calle dei Preti, 3778
Tel. 041 710 227
Mon-Sat 7am–2am
Closed Aug.
Pub-style, with subdued lighting, a wooden bar, and pop music. Happy hour daily from 8.30–9.30pm. From Oct. to the end of April, free concerts (jazz and blues)

on Fri. evenings.
Beer 2 € –2.60 €.
Café Noir (C F1)
→ *Dorsoduro,*
Calle San Pantalòn, 3805
Tel. 041 710 925
Mon-Sat 7am–2am
Along the length of the window runs a bar where you can sit and watch the passers-by. People crowd here to eat (good *panini*) and drink, and also to catch up on the foreign newspapers or surf the net (3.10 €/hr).
Beer 2.60 € –4.20 €.
Il Caffè (C E2)
→ *Dorsoduro,*
Campo Santa Margherita,
2963
Tel. 041 528 79 98
Mon-Sat 7am–1pm
Also nicknamed *caffè rosso* (red café) because of its red sign. Tables are laid out around an old bar complete with Art-Deco coffee percolator. Come here for a morning cappuccino or lunchtime *panini*. In the evening have a drink and listen to the jungle music. Lovely terrace on the square. Live music Thu. evenings with jazz or rock concerts. Cappuccino 1.80 €.
Suzie Café (C C3)
→ *Dorsoduro,*
Campo San Basegio, 1527

Tel. 041 522 75 02
Daily 7am–8pm
Live music Fri. until 2am
A good place to stop for a break, this terraced café is two paces from the Giudecca canal. Fruit juice, beers, coffee and snacks to the sound of rock or reggae music for a largely young audience. Concerts on Fri. nights.
Beer 1.80 €.

SHOPPING

Emporio Pettenello (C E2)
→ *Dorsoduro,*
Campo Santa Margherita,
2978
Tel. 041 523 11 67
Mon-Sat 9.15am–1pm,
3.45–8pm.
Closed 2 weeks in Aug.
This toy shop resembles an Aladdin's cave, packed with doting parents buying treats for their offspring. Every type of gadget: excellent puzzle section.
Capricci e Vanità (C F1)
→ *Dorsoduro,*
Calle San Pantalon, 3744
Tel. 041 523 15 04
Mon 4–7.30pm; Tue-Fri
10am–12.45pm, 4–7.30pm;
Sat 10am– 12.45pm.
Close Tue in June-July
Lovely boutiques run

by two very talented dress-makers. Delightful, quaint atmosphere. Shirts, nightdresses, lacework, household linen and a range of *pizzi* (lace from the 19th- and early 20th-centuries), embroidered silk scarves and bags decorated with pearls and gold-thread fabrics.
Torrefazione India Caffè (C E2)
→ *Dorsoduro,*
Campo Santa Margherita,
2994/5 Tel. 041 909 477
Mon-Tue, Thu-Sat
9am–1pm, 4.30–7.30pm;
Wed 9am–1pm
Coffee from all over the world, whole beans or freshly ground (1.40 € to 1.90 €/4 oz). Try Miscela nº 2, delicately flavored and mildly strong. Teas, herbal teas and teapots.
Gualti (C E2)
→ *Dorsoduro,*
Rio terrà canal, 3111
Tel. 041 520 17 31
Tue-Sun 10am–7.30pm
No Murano glass to be found here: all the jewelry is made from soft plastic. Original, brightly-colored designs with flowers or tentacles. Prices range from 16 € to 260 € (necklaces from 30 €, earrings from 42 €).

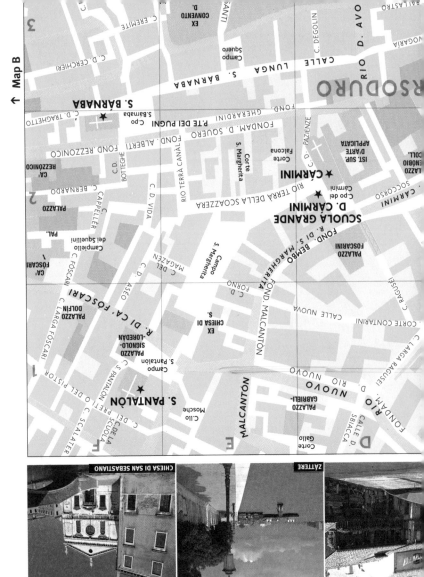

CHIESA DI SAN SEBASTIANO

ZATTERE

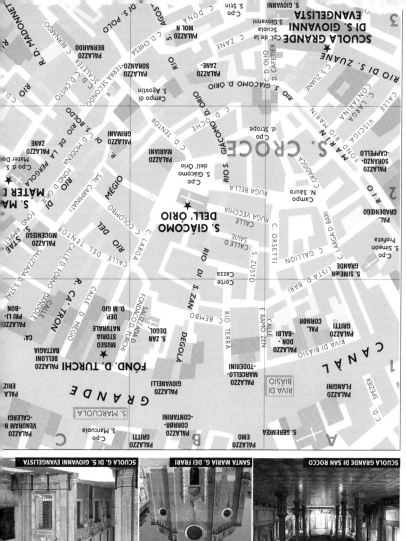
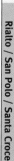

SCUOLA GRANDE DI SAN ROCCO

SANTA MARIA G. DEI FRARI

SCUOLA G. DI S. GIOVANNI EVANGELISTA

To the north of the Campo dei Carmini, the *sestiere* of San Polo begins. Some of the most beautiful religious buildings in Venice are grouped together on the Campo dei Frari, while in the nearby back streets there are numerous traditional shops, cafés and *osterie*, all attracting regulars. To the north, lovely Venetian palaces line the Grand Canal and at the east tip of San Polo, the Rialto, Venice's former trade center still boasts colorful markets and a magical arcaded bridge which takes you back to the tourist-filled main streets of San Marco.

ALLA ZUCCA

BÀCARO JAZZ

RESTAURANTS

Due Colonne (D B3)
→ San Polo,
Calle della Chiesa, 2343
Tel. 041 524 06 85
Daily 8am–2pm, 7–11pm.
Closed in Aug. and 20 days end Dec/beginning Jan.
Pizzas topped with fresh mozzarella, seasonal vegetables, *prosciutto di Parma*... Served in an old wood-paneled room, or outside on the terrace.
À la carte 10.50 €.

Frary's (D B3)
→ San Polo,
Fondamenta dei Frari, 2559
Tel. 041 720 050
Mon & Wed-Sun 10am–midnight
Two chefs, one Iraqi, the other Jordanian, create authentic middle-eastern dishes here: moussaka, falafel, kebabs, couscous (meat or vegetarian), and pastries. Excellent *vino della casa* (house wine).
À la carte 18 €.

Shri Ganesh (D AB3)
→ San Polo, Calle de'll Olio o del Cafetier, 2426
Tel. 041 719 804
Mon-Tue & Fri-Sun 12.30–2pm, 7.30pm–11pm;
Thu 7.30pm–11pm.
Delicious *shaki korma*, *tandoori* (chicken, lamb) and vegetarian curry in the only Indian restaurant in Venice. Pleasant terrace. À la carte 20.50 €.

La Zucca (D C2)
→ Santa Croce,
Calle del Megio, 1762
Tel. 041 524 15 70
Mon-Sat 11.30am–3pm, 7pm–midnight
1001 different ways to cook zucchini (*zucca*): gratin, in pasta, fried. Also serves middle-eastern inspired dishes: beef with chickpeas and couscous. Italian wines.
À la carte 25.80 €.

Bàcaro Jazz (D F3)
→ San Marco 5546, facing the Fóndaco dei Tedeschi,
Tel. 041 528 52 49
Mon-Tue & Thu-Sun noon–2am
Stop here for a drink or meal at any hour of the day. Multi-colored paper lanterns hang outside, and lights made out of colanders hang inside. Varied menu: calamari and fried zucchini, pasta, meat, fish and delicious home-made tiramisu.
À la carte 21 €.

Da Fiore (D C3)
→ San Polo,
Calle del Scaleter, 2202/A
Tel. 041 721 308
Tue-Sat 12.30–2.30pm, 7.30–10pm
The epitome of Venetian cuisine, serving the stars of the big screen during

BAR SAN STIN

LABORATORIO ARTE & COSTUME

LEGATORIA POLLIERO

the Mostra. Sea bass with balsamic vinegar marinade and other delicious fish dishes. À la carte 82 €.

ICE CREAM PARLORS

Alaska (D A2)
➔ Santa Croce,
Calle larga dei Bari, 1159
Tel. 041 715 211
Daily 11am–11pm.
Closed Dec-Jan
Welcome to the icy world of Carlo Pistacchi: brightly colored, Jamaican-style setting and reggae music. Ice cream in unusual flavors: green melon, carrot, fennel, celery: 1 € –1.80 €.

BACARI, CAFÉS, MUSIC VENUES

Antica Osteria Ruga Rialto (D E3)
➔ San Polo, Ruga Vecchia San Giovanni, 692
Tel. 041 521 12 43
Tue-Sun 11am–midnight
Stop for an apéritif, Venice-style. Huge old casks, exposed beams, wooden bar. Try sarde in saor or the frittura mista di pesce (fried mixed fish). Beer 1.50 € –3.10 €.

Cantina Do Mori (D E3)
➔ San Polo,
Calle dei Do Mori, 429
Tel. 041 522 54 01
Mon-Sat 8.30am–8.30pm

Closed 3 weeks in Aug.
The best prosecco in the oldest bacari in Venice (1462). Vassoio misto (selection of various dishes) and over a hundred different types of wine, by the glass, bottle or jug. From 7.80 € per 75 cl.

Bar San Stin (D B3)
➔ San Polo,
Campo San Stin, 2532
Tel. 041 528 53 34
Mon-Sat 7am–10pm
Quench your thirst on the colorful Campo de San Stin. Fruit juice, espresso, cappuccino, alcoholic drinks – take a relaxing break on the terrace, under the shade of a large umbrella.

Caffè dei Frari (D B3)
➔ San Polo,
Fondamenta dei Frari, 2564
Tel. 041 524 18 77
Mon-Sat 7.30am–midnight
Painted sign, ancient tiles, a mezzanine, old ceiling fans, atmospheric music... a great retro-style café at the foot of the Ponte dei Frari, the perfect place for a coffee or a sandwich. The bar spills onto the street allowing you to enjoy the evening breeze. Cocktails. Beer 3.70 €.

Pizzeria Video Jazz Club Novecento (D D3)

➔ San Polo,
Campiello del Sansoni, 900
Tel. 041 522 65 65
Tue–Sun 11.30am–3pm,
7pm–2am
In summer this is a classic pizzeria with a pleasant terrace; the rest of the year, it offers excellent live jazz (from New Orleans to fusion) on Tue. evenings. Concerts 5.20 €, beer from 4 €.

SHOPPING

Laboratorio Arte & Costume (D C3)
➔ San Polo, Calle del Scaleter, 2235 and 2199
Tel. 041 524 62 42
Mon-Sat 10am–12.30pm,
3–6.30pm
Authentic masked carnival costumes for sale or to rent. Each costume is made-to-measure and created using traditional materials (feathers and pearls of the period). For a complete costume with all accessories it will cost from 515 € to 1,600 €.

Alberto Sarria (D E3)
➔ San Polo, Fuga Vecchia San Giovanni, 777
Tel. 041 520 72 78
Mon-Sat 10am–7pm; Sun 11am–5pm (summer only)
The most beautiful masks in the city, made from papier-mâché or leather,

using traditional techniques. Original designs made to order. from 7.75 € to 517 €.

Mama Afrika (D A2)
➔ Santa Croce,
Calle Larga dei Bari, 973
Tel. 041 710 001
Mon-Sat 10am–1pm,
3.30–8pm
A little taste of Africa in Venice. Beautiful books, statuettes, jewelry, musical instruments and music which you can listen to before buying.

Legatoria Polliero (D B4)
➔ San Polo,
Campo dei Frari, 2995
Tel. 041 528 51 30
Mon-Sat 10.30am–1pm,
3.30–7.30pm
Their specialties: carta marmorizzata (marbled paper) and traditional book-binding in real leather. Diaries, frames, notebooks... Expensive, but excellent quality.

Giacomo Rizzo (D F3)
➔ Cannaregio, Salizzada San G. Crisostomo, 5778
Tel. 041 522 28 24
Mon-Tue & Thu-Sun 8.30am–1pm, 3.30–7.30pm;
Wed 8.30am–1pm
Fresh, handmade pasta in a variety of shapes, colors and unusual flavors (curaçao, cocoa, blueberry):
2 € –4.70 €/250 g.

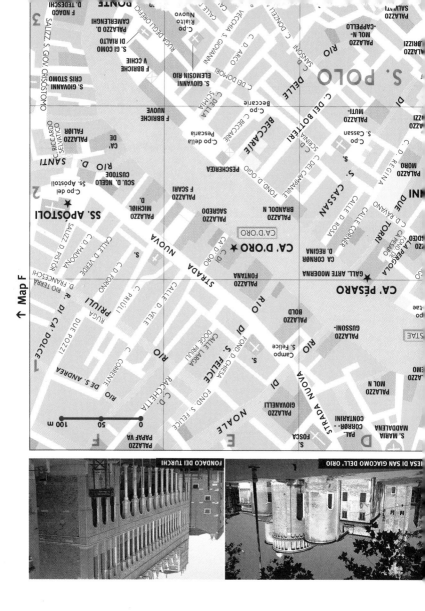

CHIESA DEI SANTI APOSTOLI

CA' D'ORO

estored the building in Venetian-Byzantine style. n 1924 the Natural History Museum opened here.

★ Santa Maria Mater Domini (**D** C2)
➔ Santa Croce, Campo
Santa Maria Mater Domini
hu-Fri 10am–noon
onstructed between two
xisting buildings, as were
any of Venice's small
hurches, the Renaissance-
nfluenced façade is made
om Istrian stone and
ttributed to Sansovino.
here are also remains of
everal Byzantine buildings
n this campo.

★ Ca' Pesaro (**D** D2)
➔ Santa Croce,
ondamenta Pesaro, 2076

Oriental Art: Tel. 041 524 11 73
Modern Art: Tel. 041 72 11 27
Tue-Sun 9am–2pm
This is one of Europe's
major Oriental art collections
located in a palace which is
a triumph of Venetian-
baroque design (1679).
Amazing Japanese costu-
mes, articles and textiles
from the Edo period (1600–
1868). Next door the Modern
Art Museum has works by
Klimt, Rodin, Matisse,
Calder and Italian paintings
from the late 1800s.

**★ Ponte di Rialto/
Rialto Bridge** (**D** F3)
The first of Venice's stone
constructions (1591) to span
the Grand Canal and, until
the 19th century, the only

link between the two
banks. The ambitious
project carried out by the
aptly named Antonio Da
Ponte also paved the way
for work by Sansovino and
Michelangelo. There are
6,000 pilings for one arch
(25ft in height) allowing
galley ships to pass under it.

**★ Chiesa dei Santi
Apostoli** (**D** F2)
➔ Cannaregio,
Campo dei Santi Apostoli
Tel. 041 523 82 97
Daily 7.30-11.30am, 4.30-7pm
The tall bell tower, with its
onion-shaped dome, is
the only one of its kind
in Venice (18th century).
The main attraction is the
16th-century Corner chapel

by Mauro Codussi, which
houses a dramatic painting
by Tiepolo (Communion of
St Lucia, 1748) and Manna
from Heaven by Veronese.

★ Ca' d'Oro (**D** E2)
➔ Cannaregio,
Calle di Ca' d'Oro, 3932
Tel. 041 523 87 90
Mon 8.15am–1.30pm;
Tue-Sun 8.15am-6.15pm
Finely chiseled loggias,
ogival windows, this is the
loveliest example of
Oriental-influenced Gothic
(1440), created by Bon and
Giovanni. In 1916 Baron
Franchetti donated the
palace and his collection
to the city: Venetian and
Tuscan schools, Gothic
furniture, Flemish tapestries.

SCUOLA LEVANTINA

CAMPO DI GHETTO NUOVO

★ Ponte
dei Tre Archi (E A2)
Despite the elegance of
this three-arched bridge
(1688), it was never copied
as it blocked both the
traffic and the view from the
canal toward the Lagoon.

★ Palazzo Labia (E C4)
→ *Cannaregio,*
Campo San Geremia, 275
Tel. 041 78 12 03
Wed-Fri 3–4pm, by appt
Three of the *palazzo*'s
façades, each very different
from the other, overlook
the *campo*, the Cannaregio
canal and the Grand Canal.
The palace's ballroom was
decorated by Tiepolo: the
large fresco depicts less
Cleopatra's life than the

wealth of the Labias, rich
Catalan merchants who
became part of Venetian
aristocracy and wanted a
palace that would reflect
their wealth and power.

★ Chiesa
di San Marcuola (E D4)
→ *Cannaregio,*
Campo San Marcuola
Tel. 041 71 38 72 Mon-Sat
9.30am–noon, 5–6.30pm
The 18th-century brick
façade (unfinished) was
built opposite a quiet *calle*
of gondolas on the Grand
Canal. The altar, by
Morlaiter (sculptor of the
main altar of the Salute),
contrasts with its plain
single nave. San Marcuola,
whose name is an odd

contraction of the saints
Ermagora and Fortunato to
whom it is dedicated, also
houses a *Last Supper* by
Tintoretto.

★ Ca'
Vendramin-Calergi (E E4)
→ *Cannaregio,*
Calle Vendramin, 2040
Tel. 041 529 71 11
Daily 9am–12.30am (casino)
With alternating columns
and twin-bay windows,
this spectacular, perfectly
balanced façade is often
considered to be the finest
example of Renaissance
architecture in Venice.
Built by Mauro Codussi in
the 16th century, it became
a style-model for 200 years.
It was once home to

Wagner, who died here on
February 13, 1883. Since
1946, the palace has
housed the winter casino.

★ Chiesa degli Scalzi
(E B1)
→ *Cannaregio, Ponte degli
Scalzi, 54*
Tel. 041 71 51 15
Mon-Sat 7-11.45am, 4-6.45pm
Sun 7.30am–12.30pm
The majesty of this façade,
punctuated with columns
and statue-filled alcoves,
contrasted sharply with the
poverty of the barefoot
(scalzi) Carmelites who
lived here. The equally
ornate baroque interior
(1656), with its multi-
colored marble and gilding
incurred bomb damage in

E

Nearly a third of the Venetian population is concentrated in Cannaregio. It is the largest sestiere after Castello. It is also away from the incessant bustle of the Rialto, and so reveals a more authentic side of Venice with quiet back streets, wide canals, laundry hung out to dry at the windows and sleeping Venetian cats. Past the vast Fondamenta, filled with typical Italian canal-side restaurants, the Jewish quarter (Ghetto Vecchio and Ghetto Nuovo) has the only six- to eight-storey buildings in Venice. Further north, close to the Canale delle Fondamenta Nuove, there are several architectural gems hidden away. Save some time to find them.

ANTICA MOLA

VINI DA GIGIO

RESTAURANTS

Iguana (**E** F3)
→ *Cannaregio, Fondamenta della Misericordia, 2515*
Tel. 041 713 561
Daily 6.30pm–2am (plus Sun lunch 11.30am–3pm)
Mayan theme throughout in this café-restaurant: parrots, multicolored lanterns and Mexican cooking. *Burritos, tortillas* (cheese or meat) and a range of *enchiladas*. À la carte 16 €.

Gam Gam (**E** C3)
→ *Cannaregio, Calle del Ghetto Vecchio, 1122*
Tel. 041 715 284
Mon-Thu & Sun noon–10pm; Fri noon–3pm
At the entrance to the old ghetto, this is the only kosher restaurant in Venice to open onto the Canal di Cannaregio. Platters of mixed starters, meat, hummus, couscous and fish made according to traditional Jewish recipes. Wine by the glass or by the jug. À la carte 18 €.

Antica Mola (**E** D2)
→ *Cannaregio, Fondamenta Ormesini, 2800*
Tel. 041 717 492
Daily noon–midnight. Closed Wed in August and Wed off season
Charming terrace on the Canal della Misericordia; inside, the beamed restaurant is decorated with old posters. Fish risotto, marinated sardines, *tagliolini* with salmon, *fritta mista*. Good choice of desserts and wines. À la carte 20 €.

Bentigodi (**E** D3)
→ *Cannaregio, Calle Sele, 1423* Tel. 041 716 269
Mon-Sat 10.30am–3pm, 6–11pm. Closed in Jan.
A great place where you can eat amongst the locals. Venetian cooking, with imagination: *branzino e melograno* (sea bass with pomegranate) won't be seen on many menus. Known for its good cellar. À la carte 26 €.

Palazzina (**E** C3)
→ *Cannaregio, Rio Terra San Leonardo, 1509*
Tel. 041 717 725
Mon-Tue & Thu 7.15pm–midnight; Fri-Sun 12.30–3.30pm, 7.15pm–midnight. Closed 2 weeks in Jan.
A *trattoria*-pizzeria in verdant setting: interior courtyard, arbor and small dining room on the canal. Pizzas (*bressaola*, Parma ham, 4 cheeses, etc.), *antipasti* (sardines, marinated salmon), home-made pasta. À la carte 30 €.

PARADISO PERDUTO

FIDDLER'S ELBOW

LUSH

Vini da Gigio (E F4)

→ Cannaregio, Fondamenta di San Felice, 3628
Tel. 041 528 51 40
Tue-Sun noon-2.30pm, 7.30-10pm. Closed in Aug and 3 weeks in Jan.
A simple but refined *trattoria* with a wide choice of quality wines (over 400 on the menu) and excellent cooking: *antipasti*, risottos, *sepia* (cuttlefish) *con polenta*. Booking strongly advised. À la carte 36 €.

PATISSERIES

Al Boscolo (E E3)

→ Cannaregio, Campiello del Anconeta, 1818
Tel. 041 720 731
Tue-Sun 7am-9pm.
Closed in July.
Delightful pastry shop where you can quench your thirst after enjoying crispy *fritelle*, delicious *zaletti* with raisins, *pincia* with cornmeal... Try also the house specialty: aphrodisiac chocolates.

WINE BARS, PUBS

Cantina Vecia Carbonera (E F4)

→ Cannaregio, Strada Nuova, 2329
Tel. 041 710 376
Tue-Thu 10.30am-10pm;
Fri-Sun 10.30am-midnight
Good bread, smooth wines and tasty cheeses in a bistro that is a favorite meeting place for groups of friends and romantic couples alike.

Do Colonne (E D3)

→ Cannaregio, Rio Terrà del Cristo, 1102
Tel. 041 524 04 53
Mon-Sat 7am-3pm, 4-9pm
Closed Tue in winter and Sun in summer.
Family-run Venetian wine bar with a very attractive cellar (Tregolino rosse, Pino nero etc.) and reasonable prices. Some food available. 0.50 €-2 € the glass of wine.

Alla Fontana (E B3)

→ Cannaregio, Fondamenta Cannaregio, 1102
Tel. 041 715 077 Mon-Sat 8.30am-2.30pm, 6-10pm;
Wed 8.30am- 2.30pm
A bistro-like *osteria* that opens onto the quays with beams, hexagonal floor tiles and 7 tables outside. Fruity Venetian wines, *ciccheti* and excellent fish specialty.

Paradiso Perduto (E F3)

→ Cannaregio, Fondamenta della Misericordia, 2540
Tel. 041 720 581
Mon, Thu & Sat 7pm-2am;
Sun noon-2am
A paradise that is certainly not lost on night-owls who like to pile into this rectangular dining room. Varied music: jazz, tango, reggae, recorded or live. Beer 2.50 €-3.70 €.

Fiddler's Elbow (E F4)

→ Cannaregio, Corte dei Pali, 3847
Tel. 041 523 99 30
Daily 5.30pm-midnight
The result of twinning Dublin and Venice (the owner also has a Venetian-style *bacaro* in the center of Dublin), this Irish pub is packed with Venice's foreign students. Stout, cider, Irish coffee and cable television (in English). Beer 2 €-3.90 €.

SHOPPING

Lush (E F4)

→ Cannaregio, Strada Nuova, 3822
Tel. 041 24 11 200
Mon 3.30-7.30pm; Tue-Sun 10am-7.30pm (8pm Sat)
Soaps, bath oils, cosmetics. The products are all made using fruit and vegetable extracts.

Mori e Bozzi (E E3)

→ Cannaregio, Rio terrà Maddalena, 2367
Tel. 041 715 261
Mon-Sat 9.30am-12.30pm, 3.30-7.30pm (also Sun in fall and spring)
Italian-designed leather goods, with Giancarlo Paoli at the helm: original and colorful shoes and bags to suit all occasions. For a young(ish) clientele.

Esperienze (E C3)

→ Cannaregio, Ponte delle Guglie, 326/B
Tel. 041 721 866
Mon-Sat 9.30am-7.15pm;
Sun 10am-7pm, 10am-9pm
When jewelry-designer Visma Sara meets Murano glass, wonders happen in the form of pins and necklaces in asymmetric shapes and bright colors.

Stamperia del Ghetto (E C3)

→ Cannaregio, Calle del Ghetto Vecchio, 1185/A
Tel. 041 275 02 00 Sun-Fri 10am-6pm (5pm in winter)
Popular meeting place for Jewish people from all over the world. Old engravings and works by contemporary artists, carved wood, bookmarks with Hebrew characters.

La Fucina del Ferro Battuto (E F4)

→ Cannaregio, Strada Nuova, 4311
Tel. 041 522 24 36
Mon-Fri 9.30am-7.30pm;
Sat-Sun 10am-1pm, 2.30-7.30pm
Venetian lanterns in wrought iron and blown glass in all shapes, sizes and colors.

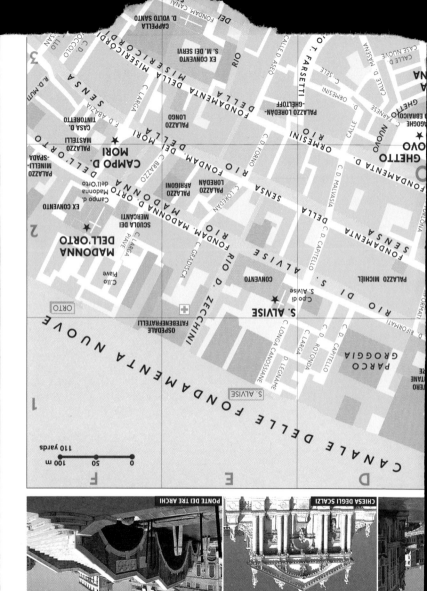

CHIESA DI SANT' ALVISE

CHIESA D. MADONNA DELL' ORTO

CAMPO DEI MORI

915; all that remains of Tiepolo's work is one fresco.

★ Scuola Levantina Sinagoga) (E C3)

→ *Cannaregio, Calle del Ghetto Vecchio, 1228 Tel. 041 71 53 59*

The most impressive of the Ghetto's 5 remaining *scuole* were acting as synagogues. Built in 1538 by the rich Jewish Sephardic community, it was renovated in the 17th century, probably by Longhena, the great Venetian baroque architect. Behind the heavy façade with its large windows, are rich rooms designed for worship, carved wooden columns, and a décor by Brustolon (13th century).

★ Campo di Ghetto Nuovo (E D3)

→ *Cannaregio*

For guided tours of the area, meet at the museum, Campo di Ghetto Nuovo, on Sun-Fri 10am–7pm (June-Sep) or 10am–4.30pm (Oct-May) The central square of the Jewish quarter. Residing in Venice since the 1300s, Jews found themselves assigned by Senate decree (1516) to a residential zone which was locked at night: the ghetto was named after the nearby foundry (*geto*). As the population grew, taller and taller buildings were erected, six to eight storeys high – the city's little 'skyscrapers'.

★ Chiesa di Sant'Alvise (E E2)

→ *Cannaregio, Campo Sant' Alvise, 3282 Tel. 041 275 04 62 Mon-Sat 10am–5pm; Sun 1–5pm. Closed July-Aug.*

Venice's most remote church, delightfully medieval in style (1388). The diminutive entrance seems a little lost against the plain façade; the elaborate baroque interior has a *trompe l'œil* ceiling and frescoes by Tiepolo.

★ Chiesa della Madonna dell'Orto (E F2)

→ *Cannaregio, Campo della M. dell'Orto Tel. 041 275 04 62 Mon-Sat 10am–5pm; Sun 1–5pm. Closed July-Aug.*

Elegant red-brick façade in a blend of styles: Renaissance portal, Romanesque alcoves, little Gothic arches. Tintoretto painted his most beautiful works here (e.g. *The Last Judgement*) and is buried in the chapel.

★ Campo dei Mori (E F3)

The name Mori stems from the district's Arab merchants whose *fondachi* (warehouses) were located here. Built into the wall are three 13th-century statues depicting three brothers. The most famous of them 'sior Antonio Rioba', depicted with an iron nose, was the spokesman for the Venetians in criticising the Republic.

TEATRO MÁLIBRAN ★

Corte d. Milion

PALAZZO
BRAGADÌN-
-CARABBA

PALAZZO
PISANI

**MONUMENTO A
B. COLLEONI**

PALAZZO
CAVAZZA-

Campo
S. Marina

PALAZZO
MARCELLO-

C.po
San Lio

S.

PALAZZO
GUSSONI

SALIZZADA

C.po
d. Fava

S.
MARIA

PALAZZO
RUZZINI

Campo
S. Maria
Formosa

PALAZZO
DONÀ

PALAZZO
VITTURI

**S. MARIA
FORMOSA** ★

**PALAZZO
GRIMANI** ★

CHIESA DI SANTA MARIA DEI MIRACOLI

TEATRO MALIBRAN

CHIESA DI SANTA MARIA FORM

★ **Chiesa dei Gesuiti** (**F** B1)
→ Cannaregio, Campo dei
Gesuiti Tel. 041 523 16 10
Daily 10am–noon, 4–6pm
In 1715 Rossi was commissioned to rebuild this Jesuit church to reflect the glory of the order (at a time of growing anti-Semitism). The result was a lavish baroque façade and an impressive interior: stucco, multicolored marble resembling draped fabric on the pulpit , and a huge canopy. Contains Titian's The Martyrdom of St Lawrence.

★ **Fondamenta Nuove**
(**F** D2)
→ Cannaregio
Wide canal paths (1589)

where the gardens of private houses once led down to the water. The view takes in the 'Island of the Dead' (San Michele is the site of Venice's largest cemetery since 1807.) On a clear day the Dolomite mountains are visible in the distance. Embarcation point for island crossings.

★ **Basilica dei Santi
Giovanni e Paolo** (**F** C3)
→ Castello, Campo dei Santi
Giovanni e Paolo, 6363
Tel. 041 523 59 13
Mon-Sat 8am–12.30pm,
3.30–6pm; Sun 3–8pm
A subtle blend of red brick and white stone, this huge building is one of Venice's grandest examples of

religious Gothic architecture (along with Chiesa dei Frari). Built on drained ground in the 13th century by Dominicans, it became a pantheon in the 1400s: there are monuments to 25 doges, sculpted by some of Italy's greatest masters, and in the Capella della Rosario are paintings by Bellini, Lotto, Veronese...

★ **Scuola Grande di
San Marco** (**F** C3)
→ Castello, Campo dei Santi
Giovanni e Paolo
The asymmetric, marble-inlaid façade (1495) with its broad, projecting portal and trompe l'oeil effects make this one of the most prestigious buildings on

the campo. The building now provides an unusual setting for a hospital.

★ **Monumento a
Bartolomeo Colleoni**
(**F** C3)
→ Castello, Campo dei Sar
Giovanni e Paolo
In his will in 1475 the worthy condottiere (merce nary) Colleoni bequeathed his fortune to the Serenissima on condition that a commemorative statue of himself be erect in Piazza San Marco. Sinc it was forbidden by law to erect any monument in th great square, the Senate solved its dilemma by having the splendid Renaissance sculpture

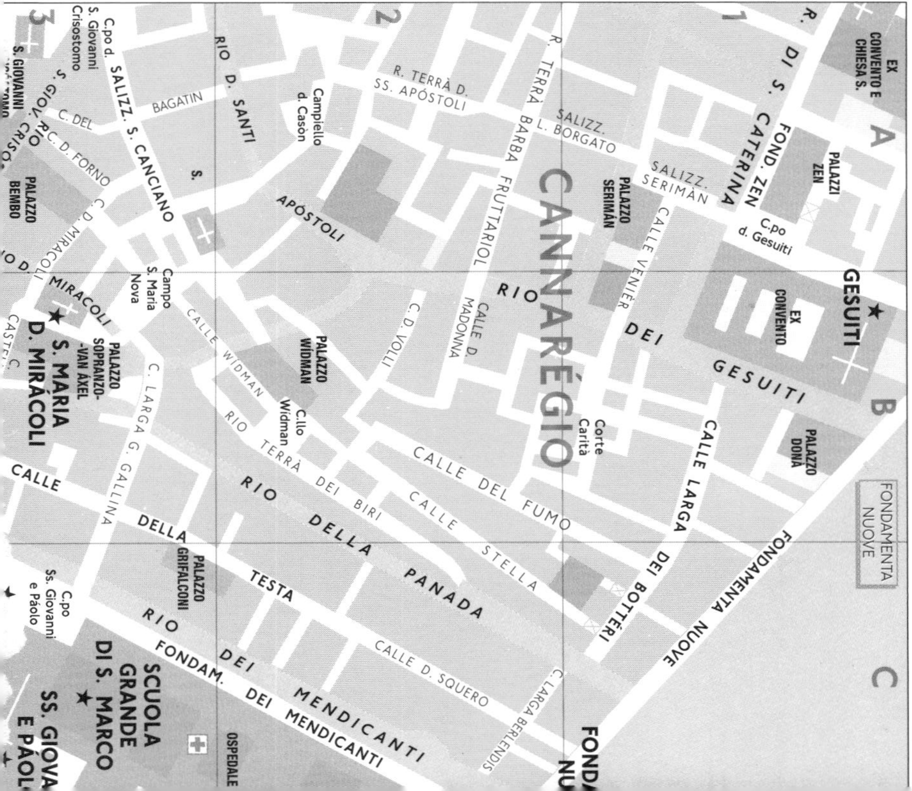

SS. GIOVA E PAOL

C.po Ss. Giovanni e Paolo

SCUOLA GRANDE DI S. MARCO

OSPEDALE

S. MARIA D. MIRACOLI

PALAZZO SOPRANZO- -VAN AXEL

PALAZZO GRIFALCONI

FONDAM. DEI MENDICANTI

CALLE D SOUERO

C. LARGA G. GALLINA

Campo S. Maria Nova

SALIZZ. S. CANCIANO

S.

BAGATIN

PALAZZO BEMBO

RIO MIRACOLI

C. DEL FORNO

S. GIOV. CRISO

S. Giovanni Crisostomo

RIO D. SANTI

APOSTOLI

Campiello d. Cason

SS. APOSTOLI

RIO TERA DEI BIRI

C.llo Widman

PALAZZO WIDMAN

CALLE WIDMAN

TESTA DELLA PANADA

RIO DELLA PANADA

CALLE STELLA

CALLE DEL FUMO

CANNAREGIO

Corte Carità

C. D. VOLLI

CALLE D. MADONNA

RIO

R. TERRA BARBA FRUTTARIOL

SALIZZ. SERIMAN

PALAZZO SERIMAN

CALLE VENIER

SALIZZ. SERMAN

L. BORGATO

R. TERRA D. APOSTOLI

DEI GESUITI

FONDA NU

C. LARGA BERLENDIS

FONDAMENTA NUOVE

CALLE LARGA DEI BOTTERI

PALAZZO DONA

EX CONVENTO

GESUITI

FOND. ZEN

C.po Gesuiti

PALAZZI ZEN

EX CONVENTO E CHIESA S.

R. DI S. CATERINA

FONDAMENTA NUOVE

3 2 1

C B A

FONDAMENTA NUOVE

CHIESA DEI GESUITI

The broad quays of the Fondamenta Nuove are reminiscent of the Záttere of Dorsoduro: waterside ice cream sellers and cafés with stunning views over the Lagoon and the island of San Michele. Taking the Fondamenta dei Mendicanti brings you out to the north of Castello and into one of Venice's major squares: Campo Santi Giovanni e Paolo, nicknamed the Campo delle Maravege (Place of Marvels) because of the amazing buildings that surround it. From there a series of busy streets lead to Campo Santa Maria Formosa where fruit and vegetable stalls stand beside lively, terraced cafés.

ALGIUBAGIÓ   AL MASCARON

RESTAURANTS

Enoteca Boldrin (F A3)
→ *Cannaregio,*
Salizzada San Canciano,
5550
Tel. 041 523 78 59
Mon-Sat 9.30am–9pm.
Closed 2 weeks in July.
One of the best venues in the city for cheap food. Pasta dishes with all kinds of sauces, main courses (*osso buco*, grilled chicken, *polenta*). À la carte 13 €.

Algiubagió (F B1)
→ *Cannaregio,*
Fondamenta Nuove, 5039
Tel. 041 523 60 84
Daily 6.30am–8.30pm.
Closed in Jan.
A restaurant-bar-cum-ice-cream parlor situated right on the canal. Splendid terrace opposite the islands of San Michele and Murano, and a lovely dining room decorated with maritime paraphernalia. Choice of pasta dishes, salads and grilled meats. Delicious homemade ice cream. À la carte 15.50 €.

Malibran (F A3)
→ *Cannaregio,*
Corte del Milion, 5864
Tel. 041 522 80 28
Daily noon–3pm, 7pm–1am
Marinated clams, gnocchi with sage, fried fish... all served in a 16th-century building opposite the Teatro Malibran. Pleasant terrace on the Corte del Milion. À la carte 26 €.

Al Mascaron (F C4)
→ *Castello,*
Calle Lunga Santa Maria
Formosa, 5525
Tel. 041 522 59 95
Mon-Sat noon-3pm, 7-11pm
Closed Dec 15 – Jan 15
A great opportunity to eat in a genuine, traditional Venetian *bacaro*. Menu changes daily, but Venetian specialties always take pride of place (delicious spaghetti with lobster, crab and various fish sauces). Beware: no credit cards. À la carte 35 €.

Fiaschetteria Toscana (F A3)
→ *Cannaregio,*
Campo San Giovanni
Crisostomo, 5719
Tel. 041 528 52 81
Mon 7.30–10.30pm;
Wed-Sun 12.30–2.30pm,
7.30–10.30pm.
Closed 2 weeks in Aug.
Superb wine list and delicious food. Choice of antipasti (swordfish *carpaccio*, baked *canestrelli*), fish risotto and delicious main courses such as John Dory with capers, Florentine-style cutlets... À la carte 39 €.

ROSA SALVA

ALLA MASCARETA

BOTTIGLIERIA COLONNA

Antiche Cantine Ardenghi (F B3)
→ Cannaregio,
Calle della Testa, 6369
Tel. 041 523 76 91
Mon-Sat 8pm–midnight
No written menu in this small restaurant (seats 20) but daily specials that depend on the whim of the chef (fried fish, eel and polenta). Dinner (incl. wine, coffee and grappa) 41 €. Booking advised.

PATISSERIES, ICE CREAM PARLORS

Zanzibar (F B4)
→ Castello, Calle del Mondo Nuovo, 3607
Tel. 034 8045 54 34
Daily 7.30am–2am (8pm in winter)
A clubhouse decorated with colorful African-style frescoes. Inside, a tiny bar plays reggae music at full volume. Attractive, sunny terrace. Ice cream and sandwiches.

Rosa Salva (F C3)
→ Castello, Campo Santi Giovanni e Paolo, 6779
Tel. 041 522 79 49
Mon-Tue & Thu-Sun 7.30am–8.30pm;
Sun 8.30am–8.30pm
The best pastries in Venice: baicoli, busolai (dried aniseed biscuits) and home-made ice

cream. From the terrace there is an unbeatable view of Santi Giovanni e Paolo.

PUBS, CAFÉS, WINE BARS

Alla Mascareta (F C4)
→ Castello, Calle Lunga Santa Maria Formosa, 5183
Tel. 034 8 04 554 34
Mon-Sat 5pm–1am
The two wine experts at this enoteca, Bianca and Enrico, have made it their business to advise customers overwhelmed by the extensive wine list. Sandwiches, panini, cold meats, cheese and ciccheti also available.

Osteria da Alberto (F B3)
→ Cannaregio, Calle larga Giacinto Gallina, 5401
Tel. 041 523 81 53
Mon-Sat 10.15am–3pm, 5.45–11pm.
Closed July 15 – Aug 8.
This famous osteria has been taken over by two young owners. Wood décor, bar serving wines, spirits and ciccheti... The ideal place to stop for an early evening drink.

L'Olandese Volante (F A4)
→ Castello, Campo San Lio, 5658

Tel. 041 528 93 49
Mon-Sat 11am–1am;
Sun 5pm–1am
A traditional Irish pub-style bar. Draught and bottled beers and a lively student crowd. In summer the terrace spills out onto the Campo. Salads and hot dishes. Beer 2.10 €–4.65 €.

Caffè all'Orologio (F C4)
→ Castello, Campo Santa Maria Formosa, 6130
Tel. 041 523 05 15
Mon-Sat 7am–11pm
Instantly recognizable by the large clockface at the front. Sit on the terrace, sip a cappuccino and admire one of the most charming campi in Venice. Coffee 2.30 €.

SHOPPING

Nicolao Atelier (F A3)
→ Cannaregio, Calle del Bagatin, 5565
Tel. 041 520 70 51
Mon-Fri 9am–1pm, 2–6pm (by appt.)
Buy or rent sumptuous carnival costumes made by professional theatrical costumiers. From 62 € per day.

Kalimala (F B4)
→ Castello, Salizzada San Lio, 5387
Tel. 041 528 35 96

Mon-Sat 9.30am–7.30pm;
Sun 11am–6.30pm (except from Nov to Jan)
Quality leather bags and purses in all shapes and sizes. Original designs and dark, subtle colors – the height of casual elegance.

Bottiglieria Colonna (F A4)
→ Castello, Calle della Fava, 5595
Tel. 041 528 51 37
Mon-Sat 9am–1pm, 4–8pm
Italian wines to suit all budgets and every occasion (from vintage Sassicaia to table wines). Gift boxes (six bottles). Also sells spirits from all over the world (ouzo, vodka, whisky).

Nave de Oro (F A2)
→ Cannaregio, Rio Terrà dei Santi Apostoli, 4657
Tel. 041 522 78 72
Mon-Tue & Thu-Sat 9am–1pm, 4–8pm;
Wed 9am–1pm
A well-known wine merchant (there are several branches throughout the city) selling Italian vintage wines on tap by the litre: you bring your own bottles and fill them up. Merlot 1.45 € per litre, Ramandolo 2 € per litre.

S. MARIA
D. VISITAZIONE

OSPEDALETTO

BARBARÍA D. TOLE

PALAZZO
MOROSINI

C. NICOLÒ M.
C. D. MOSCHE
CALLE D. CAP
RIO DI S. GIU

C. DEL CAFFETTIÈR

PALAZZO
MUAZZO

PALAZZO
CIMA-
ZON

S. GIOVANNI

S. GIOVANNI
IN LATERANO
(EX

LATERANO

RAMO CAPPELLO

PALAZZO
CAPPELLO

FONDAM. DI S. GIUSTINA

C.
S. FRANCESCO

EX CHIESA DI
S. GIUSTINA

Campo
S. Giustina

PALAZZO GRITTI
O
D. NUNZIATURA

CONVENTO DEI
MINORI

Campo
S. Francesco
d. Vigna

S. FRANCESCO
D. VIGNA
★

Campo della
Confratérnita

CASTELLO

PALAZZO
DONÀ

RGA S. LORENZO

DCO S. LORENZO

D

EX
MONASTERO

Campo
S. Lorenzo

S.
LORENZO

R. D. PIETA

SALIZZ. S. GIUSTINA

PALAZZO
DA

PALAZZO
CONTARINI

RIO DI S. FRANCESCO

R. S. FRANCESCO

C. MURION

E

F

Map A →

4

PALAZZO GRIMANI

CHIESA DI SAN FRANCESCO DELLA VIGNA

erected... in front of the Scuola di San Marco.

★ **Chiesa di Santa Maria dei Miracoli** (**F** B3)
→ *Cannaregio, Campo dei Miracoli*
Tel. 041 275 04 62
Mon-Sat 10am-5pm;
Sun 1-5pm (except July-Aug)
Bordering a *rio*, this precious Renaissance gem (1489) is the work of Pietro Lombardo. Its façade, graced by some of the most beautiful masterpieces of inlaid woodwork, is encrusted with medallions of multicolored marble. Under the unique nave, the bright light shows off the reliefs, bas-reliefs and painted coffered vaulting.

★ **Teatro Malibran** (**F** A3)
→ *Cannaregio, Corte del Milion, 5870*
When it opened in 1677, this *teatro* was the largest and most magnificent of Venice's lyric theaters. Following the success of *La Fenice* (1792), it declined in popularity. Refurbished in 1834, it was renamed after the singer Maria Malibran (1808–36).

★ **Chiesa di Santa Maria Formosa** (**F** B4)
→ *Castello, Campo Santa Maria Formosa, 5263*
Tel. 041 275 04 62
Mon-Sat 10am-5pm;
Sun 1-5pm (except July-Aug)
This three-nave church is one of Venice's oldest

sanctuaries. Mauro Codussi built his church (1492) on the foundations, giving it the form of a Latin cross. The busts of the Capello (patrons of the arts) on the double façade, show the trend for turning churches into commemorative monuments. The polyptych by Palma il Vecchio is dedicated to St Barbara, and has the features of the 'ideal woman' of Venetian 16th-century painting.

★ **Palazzo Grimani** (**F** C4)
→ *Castello, Ruga Giuffa, 4862*
Visits by appointment
Tel. 041 71 97 07
Situated at the corner of the Santa Maria Formosa canal. It is said that the

Grimani, lovers of antiques, used to exhibit their collection on the Ruga Giuffa. These works were later bequeathed to the Archeological Museum.

★ **Chiesa di San** (**F** F4)
Francesco della Vigna
→ *Castello, Campo San Francesco della Vigna*
Tel. 041 520 61 02
Daily 8am–12.30pm, 3–7pm
The grapevine (*vigna*) that on the *campo* has by now disappeared. Working to a classical model, the Palladian façade (1562–72) of this church has an architectural harmony of alternating triangles and rectangles. Look out for Veronese's altarpiece.

AIRPORT LINKS

By water taxi
→ 24 hours. Cost: 72 €
(journey approx. 20 mins)
By ACTV bus
→ Departs every 50 mins,
around 0.80 € (20 mins)
Line 5 will take you to
Piazza Roma.
By motoscafo
→ Departs every 50 mins,
around 9.80 € (journey
approx 1hr 20 mins)
To Piazza San Marco,
terminus at the Zàttere
Dorsoduro. Stops at
Murano, the Lido and
Arsenal (Castello)
By taxi
→ 24 hours. Cost: 26 €
(journey approx 20 mins)
To Piazza Roma.

MARCO POLO AIRPORT

AIRPORT LINK

VENICE BY ROAD

By taxi
For traveling outside of
the Lagoon area only,
from Piazzale Roma.
→ Station Piazzale Roma
Tel. 041 523 77 74
→ Radio Taxi
Tel. 041 936 222
By car
Cars are not permitted
on the Lagoon, and
must be left in one of the
paying parking lots at the
entrance to the city.
Parking
Parking spaces are
difficult to find and very
expensive. Many hotels
offer a 20% discount for
the Tronchetto parking lot
(minimum stay: 3 days).
Autorissima Tronchetto
→ Isola del Tronchetto
Tel. 041 520 75 55
24 hrs; 17 € per day
Autorissima Comunale
→ Piazzale Roma
Tel. 041 272 73 01
24 hrs; 18.50 € per day
Parcheggio Sant'Andrea
→ Piazzale Roma
Tel. 041 272 73 04
24 hrs; 4.20 €/2 hours
Speed limits
In Italy speed limits are
30mph in built-up areas,
55mph on highways and
80mph on freeways.
Car pounds
Beware, all badly parked
cars will be towed. To
release your car contact:
Polizia Municipale
→ Piazzale Roma
Tel. 041 274 92 98
or 041 522 45 76
By bus
Lines 2, 4, 5, 7, 12 and 19,
are run by the ACTV
company and operate
between Piazzale Roma
and Mestre.

Zàttere ai Gesuati, 780
Tel. 041 520 64 64
email: la.calcina@libero.it
Despite the popularity of
the area prices stay the
same throughout the year.
Simple but refined décor;
some rooms have magni-
ficent views of the island
of Giudecca. In season,
breakfast is served on the
terrasse giving onto the
Canal. 78 €–155 €.
Galleria (B C3)
→ Dorsoduro, Rio Terrà
Antonio Foscarini, 878/A
Tel. 041 523 24 89
In a most beautiful
Venetian-style 17th-century
palace, complete with
Venetian glass and crystal
chandeliers, fabric on the
walls and a pretty arch
doorway. The 10 rooms are
spacious and cozy. Close to
the Accademia. 92 € (82 €
without bathroom).
Locanda Al Leon
Castello, Campo St Filippo
e Giacomo, 4270

Tel 041 2770393
www.hotelalleon.com
Friendly family-run
locanda, with small but
cozy rooms, and ideally
situated a minute's walk
from St Mark's Square.
From 90 €.
Istituto Cilioto (B C2)
→ San Marco,
Calle delle Muneghe, 2976
Tel. 041 520 48 88
An old convent tucked away
in a charming flowered
courtyard – recommended
for those who like peace
and quiet. The quality of
service and spacious (air-
conditioned) rooms make
up for the modern décor
which lacks a certain charm.
Beware: there is a midnight
curfew. 82 € to 100 €
depending on the season.
**Antica Locanda Al
Gambero (A A2)**
→ San Marco,
Calle dei Fabbri, 4687
Tel. 041 522 43 84
Close to Piazza San Marco.

Has a rather old-fashioned
lobby, but the 27 recently
renovated rooms have air
conditioning, television
and telephone.
82 € (without bathroom),
123 € (with bathroom).
Tivoli (B A1)
→ Dorsoduro,
Calle Foscari 3838
Tel. 041 524 2460
Beautiful Venetian house,
large rooms and rustic
furniture. Lovely flowered
courtyard. 82 €–130 €.
Al Vagon (D F2)
→ Cannaregio,Campiello
Riccardo Selvatico, 5619
Tel. 041 528 5626
Small, well-situated hotel
with a family atmosphere.
All rooms have shower and
fan. View over Rio di Santi
Apostoli from rooms n° 25,
n° 26 and n° 29.
From 87 €. No breakfast.
Alberto Guerrato (D E3)
→ San Polo 240/A,
Calle drio la Scimia
Tel. 041 522 71 31

GONDOLAS

AIRPORT

Marco Polo airport is 7½ miles north of the city. International flights and national flights to Italy's major cities.
Travel information
Tel. 041 260 92 60
Daily 7am–midnight

Tessera

✈ **AEROPORTO MARCO POLO**

Torcello

MESTRE

SS 14

Burano

SS 14

VENETA
LAGUNA

MARGHERA

Ponte della Libertà

Murano

S. Erasmo

STAZIONE
S. LUCIA

VENEZIA

Piazzale
Roma

Lido

La Giudecca

AIRPORT

Except where otherwise indicated, prices given are for a double room with ensuite bathroom and breakfast included. Most hotels offer lower rates – up to 50% less (in Jan. especially)– out of season. Nevertheless, hotels in Venice are still expensive: for the best prices avoid those in the San Marco area.

BOOK IN ADVANCE

Despite the huge number of hotels throughout Venice, it is essential to reserve a room up to two months in advance if you are intending to visit in July, August or February (particularly during Carnival). In case of problems contact the AVA (*Associazione Veneziana Albergatori*), set up to help visitors find accommodation.

AVA
Marco Polo Airport
→ *Tel. 041 541 51 33*
Santa Lucia Station
→ *Tel. 041 715 288*
Piazzale Roma
Tel. 041 523 1397

FROM 77 €

Foresteria della Chiesa Valdese (**F** C4)
→ *Castello, Calle Lunga Santa Maria Formosa, 5170 Tel. 041 528 67 97*
A 16th-century palace which has become very popular with young travelers. Choice of twin rooms, dormitory rooms or two apartments. Excellent value for money. 51 € – 68 € (double room); 19.50 € (dormitory).
Locanda Silva (**B** B4)
→ *Castello, Fondamenta del Rimédio, 4423 Tel. 041 528 68 58*
Large, busy hotel, ideal to accommodate families.

Spacious, faultless rooms with quaint décor, and a lounge on each floor. 72 € (without bathroom).
Alex (**D** B3)
→ *San Polo, Rio Terrà Frari, 2606 Tel. 041 523 13 41*
Ideal location – close to Campo dei Frari and away from the main tourist drag. Ten basic but clean rooms. Has a pretty entrance with a wooden portico. 74 € – 85 €.
Locanda Canal (**A** C1)
→ *Castello, Fondamenta del Rimédio, 4422/C, Tel. 041 523 45 38*
Cozy hotel occupying an entire floor of a 16th-century residence at the side of a quiet canal. Good choice for small groups of travelers (7 rooms have 4 beds). Lovely view of the canal from room n°1. From 75 € (without bathroom). Generous breakfast

included in the price.
San Moisè (**B** F2)
→ *San Marco, Piscina San Moisè, 2058 Tel. 041 520 37 55*
Former convent that has retained its elegant rustic décor (high ceilings, ancient frescoes). Friendly atmosphere, good value for money and very close to the Rialto. 62 € – 232 €, depending on the season.

77 € – 102 €

Canada (**F** A4)
→ *Castello, Campo San Lio, 5659 Tel. 041 522 99 12*
Central location half-way between the lively Campo Santa Maria Formosa and the Rialto. Simple décor but clean rooms, some with private balcony. 77 € – 140 €.
Pensione La Calcina (**B** B4)
→ *Dorsoduro,*

Mestre

L A G U

Marghera

PONTE DELLA LIBERTÀ

PORTO MARGHERA

TRE ARCHI

GUGLIE

P

TRONCHETTO

FERROVIA

S. MARCUOLA

RIVA DI BIÁSIO

P.LE ROMA

P

FUSINA P

S. MARTA

S. TOMÀ

CA' REZZÓNICO

S. ÁNGELO

S. BASÍLIO

S. SAMUELE

ACCADÉMIA

SACCA FISOLA

ZÁTTERE

S. EUFÉMIA

PALANCA

Ísola della Giudecca

URBAN LINES FOR THE LAGOON

Line	Route
1	P.LE ROMA - CANÀL GRANDE LIDO
5	S. ZACCARIA - LIDO
10	S. ZACCARIA - S. SERVOLO S. LAZZARO - S. CLEMENTE
12	F. NOVE - MURANO - MAZZORBO TORCELLO - BURANO - TREPORTI - P. SABBIONI
13	F. NOVE - VIGNOLE S. ERASMO - TREPORTI
14	P. SABBIONI - LIDO - VENEZIA
16	FUSINA - ZÁTTERE
17	TRONCHETTO - LIDO
20	S. CLEMENTE - S. LAZZARO S. SERVOLO - VENEZIA
41	MURANO - F. NOVE - FERROVIA - P.LE ROMA GIUDECCA - S. ZACCARIA - F. NOVE - MURANO
42	MURANO - F. NOVE - S. ZACCARIA - GIUDECCA P.LE ROMA - FERROVIA - F. NOVE - MURANO
51	LIDO - F. NOVE - FERROVIA P.LE ROMA - S. ZACCARIA - LIDO
52	LIDO - S. ZACCARIA - P.LE ROMA FERROVIA - F. NOVE - LIDO
61	MURANO - P.LE ROMA S. ZACCARIA - LIDO
62	LIDO - P.LE ROMA FERROVIA - MURANO
61	LIDO - CASINÒ (STAG.)
62	CASINÒ - LIDO (STAG.)
71	S. ZACCARIA - MURANO - P.LE ROMA TRONCHETTO (STAG.)
72	TRONCHETTO - P.LE ROMA - MURANO S. ZACCARIA (STAG.)
82	S. ZACCARIA - GIUDECCA - TRONCHETTO - P.LE ROMA FERROVIA - RIALTO - S. MARCO - LIDO
N	NIGHT SERVICE LIDO - CANÀL GRANDE - P.LE ROMA TRONCHETTO - CANALE GIUDECCA - S. ZACCARIA
✈	S. MARCO - FONDAMENTE NOVE - AIRPORT

BACINI   STATION OPENING SOON

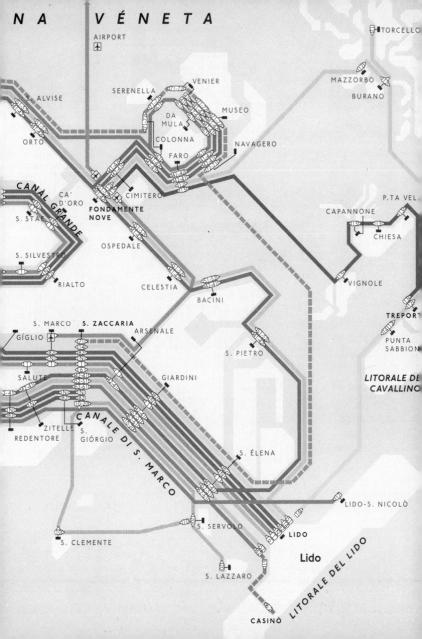

SANTA LUCIA STATION

WATER TAXI

ORIENT EXPRESS

Romantic journeys on this celebrated train, traveling through some of the most beautiful regions in Europe.
→ *Venice Simplon Orient-Express Company Tel. 01 55 62 18 00 (in Paris)*

VAPORETTO

A stunning 14th-century Venetian palace: wooden ceilings, Gothic windows, a lovely well in the garden, and, of course, all modern comforts. 130 € – 206 €.

Pensione Accademia – Villa Maravege (**B** B2)
→ *Dorsoduro, Fondamenta Bollani, 1058 Tel. 041 521 01 88*
A small guesthouse in a delightful 17th-century villa, filled with flowers and packed with charm. Four-poster beds in some rooms and slightly out-moded décoration. Peace and quiet guaranteed. 124 € – 217 €.

Santo Stafano (**B** C2)
→ *San Marco, Campo Santo Stefano,2957 Tel. 041 520 01 66*
Situated on one of the most attractive *campi* in Venice, a hotel with taste-fully decorated rooms. Highly recommended. 103 € – 232 €.

OVER 155 €

Doge (**D** A2)
→ *Santa Croce, Lista dei Bari, 1222 Tel. 041 71 72 12*
Hotel in the same area as Santa Lucia station. Classic cozy rooms and helpful staff. From 175 €.

Bel Sito (**B** E2)
→ *San Marco, Campo Santa Maria del Giglio, 2517, Tel. 041 522 33 65*
Close to the Grand Canal and La Fenice, with 36 huge, comfortable rooms. From 176 €.

Flora (**B** E2)
→ *San Marco, Calle Larga XXII Marzo, 2283/A Tel. 041 520 58 44*
Peaceful hotel for an enchanting stay close to Piazza San Marco: delightful interior court-yard where you can eat breakfast in summer. From 206 €.

PALACES

If you can't afford to spend the night in one of these gorgeous palazzi – don't worry: wear your Sunday best and treat yourself to a very expensive cappuccino there. It is often worth it.

Gritti Palace (**B** E2)
→ *San Marco, Campo Santa Maria del Giglio, 2467 Tel. 041 794 611*
A 15th-century Ogival-style palace favored by Ruskin, Hemingway and Simenon. The place to see and be seen in. 335 € – 945 €.

Danieli (**B** E2)
→ *Castello, Riva degli Schiavoni, 4196 Tel. 041 522 64 80*
Marble, sumptuous crystal chandeliers and arcaded staircases – this hotel is something of a monument. Georges Sand and Alfred de Musset conducted their love affair here. 515 € – 736 €.

VENICE BY BOAT

By vaporetto
'Vaporetto' is the general term used to refer to any type of water transport: technically speaking, a *vaporetto* is actually a large, slow-moving boat, a *motoscafo* is lower and narrower and a *motonave* is a type of ferry.
→ *15 lines running at regular intervals, 4 of them seasonal, and one night-time service (11.30pm–5.30am)*
Information
→ *ACTV (Azienda del Consorzio Trasporti Veneziano) Tel. 041 272 23 10*
Ticket sales
At major stops, tourist offices and tobacconists.
Ticket prices
→ *3.10 € per journey; 9.30 € valid for 24 hrs (students and senior citizens 5.20 €); 18 € (3 days); 31 € (7 days).*
Roll in Venice Card
→ *18 € for 3 days (students 13 €)*
Illimited access to ACTV transports, discounts in museums, restaurants...
By traghetto
Fleets of gondolas which cross the Grand Canal at reasonable rates. Seven ranks throughout the city (see the first fold-out 'Welcome to Venice').
→ *0.45 € per crossing. Times vary depending on which line is taken.*
By water taxi
Travel the length of the canal in luxurious, var-nished, wooden boats.
→ *Radio taxi Tel. 041 522 23 03 14€ (first 7 mins) then 0.25 € every 15 seconds.*

TRAINS / STATIONS

Arriving by train at the city of the Doges gives you a spectacular view of the Lagoon.

Santa Lucia

Not to be confused with the **Venezia-Mestre**, situated on the mainland, **Santa Lucia** station is built on the Lagoon, to the west of the Grand Canal.

→ *Santa Lucia travel information*
Tel. 84 88 88 088 (free)

Rail links

Routes to most major cities throughout Europe and Italy.

→ *Tickets*
Tel. 041 716 601
Daily 5.50am–9.30pm

attentive service in this elegant and rustic convent. View over the Rialto bridge from 6 of the 14 rooms. Good value for money and right in the heart of the main tourist area. 88 €–108 €.

ai do Mori (A B2)
→ San Marco, Calle Larga San Marco, 658
Tel. 041 520 48 17
Exquisite hotel in a very touristy area. Eleven small, basic but comfortable rooms, 6 with ensuite bathrooms. The nicest room is n° 11 which has exposed beams and a private terrace with views over Piazza San Marco. 93 €–119 €. No breakfast.

Locanda Fiorita (B D1)
→ San Marco, Campiello Nuovo, 3457
Tel. 041 523 47 54
Friendly little hotel on the first floor of a beautiful building on Campiello Nuovo. The rooms are small but delightful: bedheads in

green and gold wood and curtains in Venetian fabric. From 98 € (without bathroom).

103 € – 154 €

Locanda Montin (C E3)
→ Dorsoduro, Fondamenta delle Eremite, 1147
Tel. 041 522 71 51
Situated in a small ocher-colored building, opposite a lovely canal, this family run guesthouse, with flowered balconies, serves breakfast in the garden under an arbor. From 130 € (103 € without bathroom).

Agli Alboretti (B B3)
→ Dorsoduro, Rio Terrà Antonio Foscrini, 884
Tel. 041 523 00 58
A beautiful brick façade with charming rooms, a pleasant dining room and a little flowered courtyard. Only a few minutes from the Accademia. Half-board is available. 111 €–134 €.

Do Pozzi (B E2)
→ San Marco, Calle Larga XXII Marzo, 2373
Tel. 041 520 78 55
A quiet hotel on a small courtyard overlooking the busy Via XXII Marzo. High standard of service, narrow but comfortable rooms and breakfast served outside in summer. 103 €–180 € (depending on the season).

San Simon (E B4)
→ San Simeòn, Campo San Simeòn, 946
Tel. 041 71 84 90
At the edge of the Grand Canal. Quiet and refined with a pleasant terrace on the tree-lined Campo. Well-equipped rooms with good views. 103 €–197 € (depending on the season).

San Fantin (B E2)
→ San Marco, Campiello La Fenice, 1930
Tel. 041 521 523 14 01
Small and simple, family-run hotel, remarkably well situated on the Campiello

della Fenice. 144 € (10% discount July-Aug).

Locanda Sturion (D E3)
→ San Polo, Calle del Sturion, 679
Tel. 041 523 62 43
Exemplary 3-star hotel located in a beautiful 15th-century residential building overlooking the Grand Canal. Very comfortable rooms, multilingual library on Venice and old-fashioned décor.
120 €–175 €.

De l'Alboro (B D1)
→ San Marco Calle de l'Albero, 3894/B
Tel. 041 522 94 54
A modern hotel with an attractive reddish-orange façade and green shutters. Situated between the Palazzi Grassi and Contarini. Well-kept rooms. 130 €–196 €. (depending on the season).

Pausania (B A2)
→ Dorsoduro, Rio di San Barnaba, 2824
Tel. 041 522 20 83

Letters (**A, B...**) relate to the matching sections. Letters on their own refer to the spread with useful addresses. Letters followed by a star (**A★**) refer to the spread with the fold-out map and places to visit. The number (1) refers to the double page 'Welcome to Venice!' at the beginning of this guide.